The Ultimate Chinese Cookbook

111 Dishes From China To Cook Right Now

Slavka Bodic

Imprint: Independently published

Please sign up for free Balkan and Mediterranean recipes:
www.balkanfood.org

Introduction

Do you want to enjoy and celebrate the authentic Chinese flavors by cooking some delicious and savory meals at home? Then you've found a perfect read for you! This cookbook is about to introduce you to some of the most popular Chinese recipes and meals that you'll definitely love, especially if you're a spice lover. Whether you've been to China or not, you can recreate its traditional cuisine at home with the help of this comprehensive cookbook. China is popular for its unique culture, diverse languages, and amazing foods, and this book is one good way to come close to the flavorsome cuisine of this Asian country.

The Ultimate Chinese Cookbook will introduce to Chinese cuisine and its culinary culture in a way that you may have never experienced before. It brings you a variety of Chinese recipes in one place. The cookbook is great for all those who always wanted to cook Chinese food on their own without the help of a native Chinese. Based on this Chinese cuisine cookbook, you can create a complete Chinese menu of your own, or you can try all the special Chinese recipes on different occasions as well. In this cookbook, you'll find popular Chinese meals and ones that you might not have heard of formerly.

Although rice is a very important part of Chinese cuisine, there are certain formal occasions where rice isn't served at all. On these occasions, rice will only be served in the form of fried rice as a token dish when the meal is about to finish, or there are no more dishes for serving. There's also the vast importance of soups in Chinese cuisine. They're served either at the start of the meals as appetizers or even at the endings too. In this cookbook, you can also uncover:

- Facts about Chinese Cuisine
- Insights About China
- Chinese Breakfast Recipes
- The Snacks, Sides, or Appetizers
- Dumplings, Egg Rolls, And Wontons
- Chinese Soups
- Main Dishes
- Chinese Desserts and Drinks

Let's try all these Chinese Recipes and recreate a complete menu to celebrate the amazing Chinese flavors and unforgettable aromas.

Table of Contents

Why Chinese Cuisine?

There's a famous Chinese saying, "food is heaven for the people," and they have adopted it. Every single Chinese individual, irrespective of the levels of society, enjoys eating food. In turn, cooking has become a form of art over time. The Chinese are very culturally rich, and their cuisines have adopted new dishes and diverse tastes with every new dynasty. The most prominent development took place during the times of the Qing Dynasty. The most famous dinner of that time was the "Man Han Quan Xi," which was comprised of 108 top dishes from the Man & Han Cuisines.

Specifically, Chinese cuisine has encompassed of various dishes of the Chinese people and has been widely spread across the globe. There's a clear difference between taste and flavor in the food of various regions of China due to the variations in cultural and geological locations. The major regional cuisines of China are as follows:

- Cantonese Cuisine (Yue Cai)
- Shandong Cuisine (Lu Cai)
- Anhui Cuisine (Hui Cai)
- Jiangsu Cuisine (Yang Cai or Su Cai)
- Zhejiang cuisine (Zhe Cai)
- Hunan Cuisine (Xiang Cai)
- Szechuan Cuisine (Chuan Cai)
- Fujian Cuisine (Min Cai)

The four main flavors of Chinese cuisine include:

- Xiang (aroma present in dishes having a combo of taste and smell harmonious)
- Xian (natural flavor of ingredients like a taste of good-quality butter)
- You Err Bu Ni (the texture and taste of fat without stodginess or greasiness)
- Nong (concentration of a flavor or the richness of a sauce)

The Chinese meal generally embodies two or, at times, more than two main components. The primary component is a starch or a carb source, which is also called the main food in the Chinese language, i.e. Zhushi, Pinyin, which means 'the main food.' Noodles, rice, or steamed beef are included in this category. The second major component is typically comprised of side dishes with veggies, fishes, meats, etc., as the main ingredients. They're called "Cai" (which is a dish in Pinyin) in the native language of China.

Generally, rice is an integral part of Chinese cuisine. But there are certain exceptions too, like in the northern part of the country, where products like steamed bread (known as Mantou in Pinyin) and noodles etc. (which are wheat-based) are more dominant than rice, which is mostly consumed in the southern parts of the country.

China

The rising power of the East isn't new to us! China is known for many reasons; its unique culture, traditions, and cuisine are few among them. Located in East Asia, the country is inhabited by the largest population of 1.4 billion in the world. The exotic landscape and diversity of land and climate is another major attraction of this country. China holds a special place not just because of its big size and rising power but also due to its geography. It shares its borders with fourteen different countries, including India, Nepal, Pakistan, Afghanistan and Bhutan in South Asia, and Kazakhstan, Kyrgyzstan, and Tajikistan in Central Asia and North Korea, Mongolia and Russia in the Inner and Northeast Asia. It also occupies its maritime border with the Philippines, Vietnam, Japan, and South Korea. And with the new expansion global plan, China is now connected to all other parts of the world.

What I personally enjoyed in China was going out and having a range of delicious and unique meals on the streets and food places. In restaurants, the servers usually use two spoons for dividing the fish into various servings for easy consumptions. One more popular meat in Chinese cuisine is chicken. The Chinese serve every single piece of the chicken after cutting it, including the head and the gizzards too. Chinese cuisine is very fond of serving meals as a whole. The Chinese consider it as a bad omen if the chicken or fish is served without its tail or head. They deem it as bad as anything without having any defined end or beginning.

The Chinese serve their food on well-defined plates, and every individual person is served with a separate bowl of rice. The side dishes are usually served alongside them in bowls or communal plates, which are usually shared by every diner sitting on the dining table. Every single diner takes out one's food on a bite-by-bite approach using their chopsticks from the communal plates or bowls in front of them. This trait is completely opposite to the western dining approach, where the individual is served with a meal at the beginning individually.

Generally, non-Chinese aren't comfortable in allowing a diner's individual utensils for touching the communal plates or bowls due to traces of saliva or other hygienic factors. To avoid this, extra chopsticks for servings are also available. In localities where Western culture is more dominant, like Hong Kong, diners are given an individual metallic spoon for this reason. The food selected is generally consumed together with rice in an alternative approach or at times in a single bite.

Chinese cuisine has become the most sought after food in most parts of the world. It offers a wide range of recipes and the richness of their ingredients which makes Chinese dishes a must-have for everyone. They're simple and easy to make, and most of them make great use of fresh vegetables, steamed dumplings, noodles, sautéed meat, and basic sauces. Anyone who cannot tolerate tangy food fall for a Chinese meal. This cookbook is perfect for such Chinese food lovers; whether it's the morning breakfast or the late-night snack meal, try these recipes at home and enjoy their warmth with your family and friends.

Breakfasts

Chinese Shrimp Cakes

Preparation time: 10 minutes
Cook time: 20 minutes
Nutrition facts (per serving): 144 Cal (20g fat, 18g protein, 2.5g fiber)

These shrimp cakes are a classic Chinese meal, great for breakfast and for side meals. You can try these cakes with a warmed tortilla and any other bread.

Ingredients (5 servings)

1-lb. shrimp, chopped
1 small carrot, blanched and chopped
5 water chestnuts, minced
¼ cup cilantro, chopped
1 teaspoon ginger, grated
2 teaspoons Shaoxing wine
½ teaspoon salt
⅛ teaspoon white pepper
2 teaspoons oyster sauce
1 teaspoon sesame oil
¼ teaspoon sugar
1 teaspoon cornstarch
3 tablespoons oil

Preparation

Mix the water chestnuts, shrimp, carrot, ginger, cilantro, wine, white pepper, and the rest of the ingredients, except the oil, in a bowl. Add the oil to a suitable skillet and place it over medium-high heat. Make 10 patties from this mixture and sear the patties in batches in the skillet. Cook the patties for 5 minutes per side until golden brown. Serve warm.

Mung Bean Cake

Preparation time: 15 minutes

Cook time: 35 minutes

Nutrition facts (per serving): 213 Cal (20g fat, 12g protein, 7g fiber)

The Chinese mung bean cakes are prepared with beans and a mix of matcha powder, sugar, and butter, which make them an excellent breakfast serving.

Ingredients (4 servings)

9 oz. yellow mung beans, soaked

1 ½ oz. butter

1 ½ oz. vegetable oil

3 ½ oz. sugar

1 small pinch of salt

1 teaspoon matcha powder

Preparation

Add the mung beans and enough water to cover them to a pressure cooker, seal the lid, and cook for 30 minutes. Release the pressure completely and, then remove the lid. Mash the cooked beans with a fork. Sauté the beans mash with butter, vegetable oil, salt, matcha powder and sugar in a skillet for 5 minutes. Divide the fried beans mixture into mooncake molds, cover, and refrigerate for 1 hour. Serve.

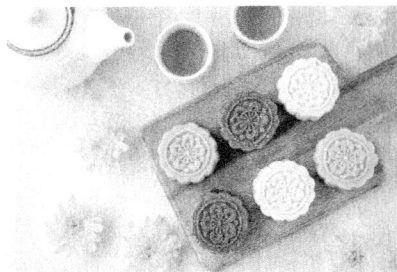

20-Minute Congee

Preparation time: 10 minutes
Cook time: 40 minutes
Nutrition facts (per serving): 217 Cal (10g fat, 15g protein, 2g fiber)

Congee is a must to have a meal in Chinese cuisine. It's prepared mainly with rice, and then different side ingredients are added for flavor enhancement.

Ingredients (4 servings)
¾ cup white rice
4 oz. pork shoulder, julienned
½ teaspoon cornstarch
1 teaspoon oyster sauce
1 teaspoon vegetable oil
7 cups of water
2 eggs, boiled, peeled, and diced
3 ginger slices
¼ teaspoon ground white pepper
Salt, to taste
Chopped scallion and cilantro

Preparation
Mix the pork with the oyster sauce, cornstarch, and vegetable oil in a bowl. Cover and marinate the pork for 20 minutes. Sear the pork in 1 teaspoon vegetable oil in a soup pot until golden brown. Keep the pork aside. Add 7 cups water, rice, ginger, white pepper and salt to a soup pot. Cover and cook the congee for 15 minutes on a simmer. Add the eggs and the pork to the congee and cook for 5 minutes on a simmer. Garnish with cilantro and scallions. Serve warm.

Chinese Tomato Egg

Preparation time: 10 minutes

Cook time: 7 minutes

Nutrition facts (per serving): 236 Cal (17g fat, 19g protein, 2g fiber)

Chinese tomato egg is a breakfast that you can serve every day with crispy bread and roasted bacon on the side.

Ingredients (4 servings)

4 tomatoes, diced

1 scallion, chopped

4 eggs

¾ teaspoons salt

¼ teaspoon white pepper

½ teaspoon sesame oil

1 teaspoon Shaoxing wine

3 tablespoons vegetable oil

2 teaspoons sugar

½ cup water

Preparation

Sauté the tomatoes and scallions with oil in a suitable wok for 2 minutes. Beat the eggs with salt, white pepper, sesame oil, wine, sugar, and water in a bowl. Pour the eggs mixture into the wok and stir cook for 5 minutes. Serve warm.

Chinese Eggs Stir Fry

Preparation time: 10 minutes

Cook time: 7 minutes

Nutrition facts (per serving): 308 Cal (10g fat, 14g protein, 0.4g fiber)

If you want something exotic and delicious on your breakfast menu, then nothing can taste better than this Chinese egg stir fry.

Ingredients (4 servings)

5 large eggs

⅛ teaspoon sugar

½ teaspoon salt

1 teaspoon Shaoxing wine

¼ teaspoon ground white pepper

¼ teaspoon sesame oil

4 teaspoons water

2 cups Chinese chives, chopped

4 tablespoons vegetable oil

Preparation

Beat the eggs with sugar, salt, wine, white pepper, water, chives, and sesame oil in a bowl. Set up a wok on medium heat and add the vegetable oil to heat. Pour the egg-wine mixture, stir, and cook for 5-7 minutes until the eggs are set. Serve warm.

Sesame Crab Cakes

Preparation time: 10 minutes
Cook time: 20 minutes
Nutrition facts (per serving): 136 Cal (4g fat, 14g protein, 2g fiber)

The famous Chinese sesame crab cakes are here to make your breakfast special. You can always serve these with crispy bacon and fried eggs.

Ingredients (4 servings)
Crab Cakes
¼ cup mayonnaise
2 scallions, chopped
2 eggs
1 tablespoon Dijon mustard
2 teaspoons Old Bay seasoning
2 teaspoons lime juice
1-lb. lump crabmeat
1 ½ cups panko breadcrumbs
2 tablespoons toasted sesame seeds
Salt and black pepper
Oil, for cooking

Tartar Sauce
½ cup mayonnaise
2 tablespoons pickles, chopped
2 tablespoons red onion, chopped
¼ cup cilantro, chopped
1 tablespoon lime juice

Preparation

Mix the crabmeat with breadcrumbs, sesame seeds, salt, black pepper, lime juice, old bay seasoning, mayonnaise, scallions, eggs, and mustard in a bowl. Make 8 equal size patties out of this mixture and refrigerate the patties for 10 minutes. Meanwhile, blend all ingredients for the tartar sauce in a blender. Sear the crab cakes in hot oil in a skillet over medium heat until golden brown. Serve warm with tartar sauce.

Ji Dan Bing

Preparation time: 15 minutes
Cook time: 10 minutes
Nutrition facts (per serving): 265 Cal (17g fat, 5g protein, 5.4g fiber)

It's about time to try some Ji dan Bing on the breakfast menu and make it taste more diverse in flavors, which is a type of pancake. Serve warm with your favorite herbs on top.

Ingredients (2 servings)
1¼ cups all-purpose flour
⅛ teaspoon salt
½ cup of warm water
Vegetable oil
4 eggs
Sweet bean sauce
Hot chili bean sauce
Hot chili oil
Toasted sesame seeds
2 scallions, chopped
1 handful cilantro, chopped
4 leaves of romaine lettuce, washed and dried

Preparation
Mix flour with ½ cup warm water and salt in a bowl for 3 minutes. Place this dough in a greased bowl, cover and refrigerate for 1 hour. Roll out the dough into a thin sheet on a working surface. Set a skillet over medium heat and grease it with cooking oil. Place the dough sheet in this skillet. Crack an egg on top and

scramble it gently. Flip the dough and cook for 10 seconds from the egg side. Mix the sweet beans, hot chili oil, and hot beans sauce in a bowl. Add this filling on top of the egg and fold the pancake. Garnish with sesame seeds, cilantro, and scallions. Enjoy.

Chinese Almond Tofu

Preparation time: 15 minutes
Cook time: 15 minutes
Nutrition facts (per serving): 242 Cal (6g fat, 9g protein, 10g fiber)

The Chinese almond tofu is a delicious morning meal you can try every day; it's best to serve with bread. You can try different fruit toppings as well.

Ingredients (4 servings)

½ lb. almond seeds
2 cups of water
4 tablespoons sugar
1 cup evaporated milk
1½ envelope gelatin
½ cup of water
½ teaspoon almond extract
Mandarins, oranges, and raspberries for the fruit salad

Preparation

Blend the almonds with water in a blender until smooth. Warm up the milk in a saucepan, and then add the almond puree, gelatin, and almond extract. Next, cook until the mixture thickens with occasional stirring. Spread the mixture in a flat pan and allow it to set. Cover and refrigerate for 4 hours and then cut into diamonds. Garnish with mandarins and fruits. Serve.

Chinese Egg Cake

Preparation time: 10 minutes

Cook time: 35 minutes

Nutrition facts (per serving): 121 Cal (10g fat, 12g protein, 2g fiber)

It's as if the Chinese menu is incomplete without these Chinese egg cake. These egg cakes are great to serve with toasted bread.

Ingredients (4 servings)

2 eggs

½ cup cake flour

3 tablespoons and 1 teaspoon castor sugar

¾ teaspoon olive oil

Warm water

Preparation

At 350 degrees F, preheat your oven. Boil water in a cooking pan and set a glass bowl in it. Add the eggs and sugar to this bowl and then beat for 15 minutes until the mixture fluffy. Remove the egg from the heat, then add the flour and oil, and then mix well. Divide this mixture into a greased muffin tray. Bake for 20 minutes in the oven and allow them to cool. Serve.

Chinese Fa Gao (Fortune Cake)

Preparation time: 15 minutes

Cook time: 25 minutes

Nutrition facts (per serving): 142 Cal (4g fat, 12g protein, 1g fiber)

Fa Gao is another Chinese morning cake recipe that you can try in breakfast. Due to its simple and quick recipe, you can easily prepare it at home as an interesting addition to lunch or a dinner.

Ingredients (6 servings)

1 cup all-purpose flour

4 oz. hot water

½ cup brown sugar

2 teaspoons baking powder

Preparation

Mix the brown sugar with hot water in a bowl. Stir in the flour and the baking powder and then mix well until smooth. Divide the batter into small tart pans and place in a steamer. Cover and steam the batter for 25 minutes. Allow the cakes to cool and then serve.

Appetizers

Chinese Pearl Meatballs

Preparation time: 10 minutes
Cook time: 20 minutes
Nutrition facts (per serving): 223 Cal (16g fat, 9g protein, 2g fiber)

Have you ever tried the Chinese pearl meatballs? Well, here's a recipe to cook them by yourself with its easy to follow ingredients.

Ingredients (6 servings)

6 dried bamboo leaves

¾ cup glutinous rice, rinsed

1-lb. ground pork

⅓ cup water chestnuts, minced

2 teaspoons ginger, minced

3 tablespoons scallions, minced

3 tablespoons cold water

2 tablespoons Shaoxing wine

2 teaspoons cornstarch

¼ teaspoon ground white pepper

½ tablespoon sesame oil

1 teaspoon of salt

½ teaspoon sugar

Preparation

Soak the bamboo leaves in water overnight and cover them with a heavy plate. Add the pork, ginger, chestnuts, water, scallions, cornstarch, wine, sesame oil, sugar, salt, and white pepper in a bowl. Soak the rice in water for 2 hours, then rinse. Cover the marinate the pork for 30 minutes. Divide the rice into a golfball sized ball and spread each into a round. Add a tablespoon of meat filling to the center of the rice and roll them around the meat. Remove the same with the remaining rice and meat filling to make more pearls. Fill a cooking pot with boiling water and set it over medium heat. Place a steamer basket over the water and spread bamboo leaves, then top them with the pearl balls. Cover and steam for 20 minutes. Serve warm.

Rice Pork Balls

Preparation time: 15 minutes
Cook time: 30 minutes
Nutrition facts (per serving): 199 Cal (8g fat, 4 protein, 1g fiber)

These rice pork balls are here to complete your Chinese menu. These pork balls can be served on all special occasions and festive celebrations.

Ingredients (6 servings)

½ cup sticky rice
1 egg
1 (1 inch) piece ginger root, minced
2 teaspoons soy sauce
Salt, to taste
4 oz. ground pork
2 tablespoons cornstarch
1 tablespoon pork stock
¼ cup of water
1 teaspoon dried goji berries

Preparation

Soak the rice in water for 2 hours in a bowl. Mix the pork stock, pork, water, salt, soy sauce, ginger, cornstarch, and goji berries in a bowl. Divide the mixture into meatballs and coat these balls with rice. Fill a cooking pot with water and set a steamer basket inside. Boil the water and spread the balls in the basket. Cover and steam these balls for 30 minutes. Serve warm.

Szechuan Edamame

Preparation time: 10 minutes

Cook time: 11 minutes

Nutrition facts (per serving): 141 Cal (4g fat, 12g protein, 1.1g fiber)

Here comes a Chinese side meal that's beloved by all. The Szechuan edamame is served with variety of entrées.

Ingredients (4 servings)

1 (16 oz.) package frozen edamame

2 teaspoons sesame seeds

3 tablespoons white sugar

2 tablespoons soy sauce

2 teaspoons olive oil

1 teaspoon red pepper flakes

Preparation

Fill a cooking pot with boiling water and soak the edamame in the water for 6 minutes. Transfer the edamame to a salad bowl. Sauté the edamame with olive oil in a skillet for 5 minutes. Stir in sugar, sesame seeds, soy sauce, and red pepper flakes. Mix well and serve.

Shrimp Balls

Preparation time: 15 minutes

Cook time: 20 minutes

Nutrition facts (per serving): 196 Cal (6g fat, 13g protein, 2g fiber)

These shrimp balls are popular Chinese snacks enjoyed all over the world. They deliver a delightful mix of shrimp filling inside spring roll wraps.

Ingredients (4 servings)

1 lb. shrimp, shelled, and deveined

1 egg white, beaten

1 teaspoon salt

1 teaspoon sugar

1 tablespoon cornstarch

½ teaspoon sesame oil

3 dashes white pepper powder

8 pieces spring roll wrapper

Preparation

Blend the shrimp with the egg white, salt, sugar, cornstarch, sesame oil, and white pepper in a bowl. Cut the roll wrappers into strips and keep them in a bowl. Make small meatballs from the shrimp mixture and wrap them with the roll wrapper strips. Heat the oil in a suitable deep pan and deep fry the shrimp ball until golden brown. Serve warm.

Koya Dofu

Preparation time: 5 minutes
Cook time: 13 minutes
Nutrition facts (per serving): 231 Cal (11g fat, 8g protein, 0.3g fiber)

Koya dofu (tofu) make a great serving if you're looking for a quick snack to make. Serve these seared sliced with some noodles.

Ingredients (2 servings)
1 Koya tofu, sliced
1 Katakuriko
2 tablespoons vegetable oil
3 tablespoons tomato ketchup
1 tablespoon soy sauce
2 teaspoons sugar
1 cucumber, peeled and sliced

Preparation
Squeeze the tofu and slice it. Coat the tofu slices with the Katakuriko. Mix the tomato ketchup, soy sauce, and sugar in a bowl. Add oil to a skillet and sear the dofu for 4-5 minutes per side. Stir in the prepared sauce and cook it for 3 minutes on a simmer. Garnish with cucumber. Serve warm.

Coconut Shrimp

Preparation time: 15 minutes
Cook time: 10 minutes
Nutrition facts (per serving): 230 Cal (12g fat, 20g protein, 1.4g fiber)

If you haven't tried the coconut shrimp before, then here comes a simple and easy to cook recipe that you can easily prepare and cook at home in no time with minimum efforts.

Ingredients (4 servings)

1 lb. shrimps
¼ cup all-purpose flour
1 teaspoon cornstarch
¼ teaspoon baking powder
¼ teaspoon baking soda
¼ teaspoon salt
¼ teaspoon garlic powder
¼ teaspoon onion powder
¼ cup ice water
½ cup coconut flakes
Peanut oil for frying

Preparation

Whisk the flour, cornstarch, baking powder, baking soda, salt, garlic powder, and onion powder in a bowl. Dredge the shrimp through the flour mixture and then dip in the water. Coat the shrimp with coconut flakes. Deep the fry the shrimp in a suitable wok filled with oil at 350 degrees F, until golden brown. Transfer these shrimps to a plate lined with a paper towel. Serve warm.

Wok Fried Peanuts

Preparation time: 15 minutes

Cook time: 2 minutes

Nutrition facts (per serving): 175 Cal (9g fat, 1g protein, 2g fiber)

Have you ever tried these wok-fried peanuts? Well, here's a recipe to cook them by yourself with its easy to follow ingredients.

Ingredients (6 servings)

6 oz. shelled raw peanuts

2 tablespoons coconut oil

Sea salt, to taste

Preparation

Sauté the peanuts with oil and salt in a suitable wok for 2 minutes. Serve.

Coconut Mochi

Preparation time: 15 minutes

Cook time: 15 minutes

Nutrition facts (per serving): 158 Cal (12g fat, 7g protein, 2g fiber)

These simple, quick and easy to make coconut mochi have no parallel. If you have some peanuts, rice, and other ingredients at home, then you can prepare it in no time.

Ingredients (8 servings)

Dough

1 ½ cups sweet rice flour

¼ cup cornstarch

¼ cup caster sugar

1 ½ cups coconut milk

2 tablespoons coconut oil

Filling

½ cup roasted peanuts, chopped

½ cup coconut flakes, chopped

3 tablespoons sugar

1 tablespoon melted coconut oil

Coconut Peanut Mochi

A large piece of wax paper

1 cup coconut flakes, chopped

16 small paper cupcake cups

Preparation

Layer an 11x11 cake pan with wax paper and brush with vegetable oil. Whisk the rice flour, sugar, cornstarch, coconut oil, and coconut milk in a bowl. Boil water in a suitable cooking pot, place the steam rack inside and add the dough to the steamer. Cover and cook for 15 minutes in the steamer, then allow the dough to cool. Meanwhile, mix the peanuts with 1 tablespoon coconut oil, sugar, and coconut flakes in a bowl. Spread the prepared dough in the prepared pan and cut it into 14 squares. Add a tablespoon of the filling at the center of each square. Pinch the edges of each square and roll it into a ball. Coat all the balls with coconut flakes and place them in the cupcake cup. Leave them for 20 minutes. Serve.

Sesame Balls

Preparation time: 10 minutes

Cook time: 20 minutes

Nutrition facts (per serving): 174 Cal (3g fat, 1g protein, 3g fiber)

Have you tried the famous sesame balls? If you haven't, now is the time to cook these delicious balls at home using simple and healthy ingredients.

Ingredients (12 servings)

1 ½ cups glutinous rice flour

⅓ cup granulated sugar

¼ cup boiling water

¼ cup water

7 oz. lotus paste or red bean paste

¼ cup sesame seeds

4 cups peanut oil for frying

Preparation

Mix sugar, ¼ cup rice flour, and ¼ cup warm water in a bowl and leave for 5 minutes. Stir in the remaining water and the remaining rice flour. Mix well, cover the dough, and leave it for 30 minutes. Meanwhile, make 8 small balls from the lotus paste. Divide the prepared dough into 8 pieces and spread each piece of dough into a round. Place one lotus paste ball at the center of each dough round and wrap it around the ball. Roll to smooth out the balls, and then coat them with sesame seeds. Add 4 cups of oil to a deep pan and heat it to 320 degrees F. Deep fry the sesame balls until golden brown. Serve.

Salads

Tofu Avocado Salad

Preparation time: 10 minutes
Nutrition facts (per serving): 191 Cal (7g fat, 8g protein, 6g fiber)

Here's a simple Chinese tofu avocado recipe made from silken tofu and soy sauce dressing. Serve this salad with noodles or rice.

Ingredients (2 servings)

7 oz. silken tofu, sliced

1 ripe avocado, peeled and sliced

2 garlic cloves, grated

1 teaspoon ginger, grated

2 tablespoons light soy sauce

1 teaspoon sesame oil

½ teaspoon sugar

½ teaspoon Chinese black vinegar

¼ teaspoon white pepper

2 teaspoons water

Salt, to taste

1 scallion, chopped

Preparation

Toss tofu with the rest of the salad ingredients in a salad bowl. Mix well and serve. Enjoy.

Chinese Cucumber Salad

Preparation time: 10 minutes

Cook time: 2 minutes

Nutrition facts (per serving): 203 Cal (4g fat, 9g protein, 1g fiber)

Make this Chinese cucumber salad in no time and enjoy it with some garnish on top. Adding a drizzle of sesame seeds on top makes it super tasty.

Ingredients (2 servings)

6 garlic cloves, minced

3 tablespoons oil

2 English cucumbers, sliced

1 ½ teaspoon salt

1 teaspoon sugar

⅛ teaspoon MSG

¼ teaspoon sesame oil

1 tablespoon rice vinegar

Preparation

Sauté the garlic with oil in a suitable wok for 30 seconds. Stir in the sugar, MSG, sesame oil, rice vinegar, and salt. Cook for 1 minute and then toss in the cucumber. Mix well and serve.

Chinese Tofu Salad

Preparation time: 15 minutes
Nutrition facts (per serving): 247 Cal (4g fat, 11g protein, 4g fiber)

The famous Chinese tofu salad with a sesame sauce on the side is a staple on the Chinese menu. Try to prepare it at home with these healthy ingredients and enjoy.

Ingredients (4 servings)
1 cup red bell pepper, julienned
1 cup red onion, sliced
1 cup carrot, julienned
1 cup cucumber, julienned
1 cup celery, julienned
8 oz. spiced tofu, shredded
1 tablespoon light olive oil
1 teaspoon garlic, minced
1 ½ teaspoons sugar
¼ teaspoon ground white pepper
2 tablespoons light soy sauce
1 tablespoon Chinese black vinegar
1 teaspoon sesame oil
1 tablespoon toasted sesame seeds
¼ cup cilantro, chopped

Preparation
Toss the shredded tofu with the rest of the salad ingredients in a salad bowl. Serve.

Dragon Spinach Salad

Preparation time: 10 minutes
Nutrition facts (per serving): 213 Cal (11g fat, 5g protein, 1g fiber)

Best to serve as a healthy side meal, this Chinese spinach salad with dragon fruit is loaded with nutrients.

Ingredients (4 servings)
Dressing
4 tablespoon rice wine vinegar

3 tablespoon soy sauce

2 teaspoons olive oil

2 teaspoons sesame oil

2 teaspoons honey

Salt and black pepper, to taste

Salad
1 cup dragon fruit, cubed

3 cups fresh baby spinach

½ cup sliced tomatoes

2 teaspoons sliced pickled ginger

Preparation
In a small bowl, add all the ingredients and beat until well combined. In a large serving bowl, add all the ingredients for salad and mix well. Pour the dressing and toss to coat well. Serve immediately.

Chinese Seaweed Salad

Preparation time: 10 minutes
Cook time: 16 minutes
Nutrition facts (per serving): 261 Cal (3g fat, 5g protein, 1g fiber)

The Chinese seaweed salad is a great delight that you can easily prepare at home. The salad is fairly easy to make and doesn't require complicated cooking techniques.

Ingredients (4 servings)
12 oz. fresh kelp
4 garlic cloves, minced
3 thin ginger slices, minced
3 Thai chilies, sliced
2 scallions, chopped
3 tablespoons vegetable oil
1 tablespoon Sichuan peppercorns
1 ½ teaspoon sugar
2 teaspoons Chinese black vinegar
2 ½ tablespoon light soy sauce
1 teaspoon oyster sauce
½-1 teaspoon sesame oil, to taste
¼ teaspoon salt
¼ teaspoon five-spice powder
1 tablespoon cilantro, chopped

Preparation

Boil the kelp in a pot filled with water for 5 minutes in a cooking pot. Drain the kelp and rinse it under the cold water. Mix the ginger, garlic, Thai chilies, and scallion in a bowl. Sauté the garlic mixture and peppercorns with 3 tablespoons oil in a saucepan for 10 minutes. Stir in the vinegar, sugar, soy sauce, salt, sesame oil, five-spice powder, and oyster oil. Add cilantro and scallions and then sauté for 1 minute. Pour this sauce over the boiled kelp leaves. Serve warm.

Dumplings, Wontons and Egg Rolls

Vegetable Dumplings

Preparation time: 15 minutes
Cook time: 32 minutes
Nutrition facts (per serving): 149 Cal (1g fat, 9g protein, 0.1g fiber)

Vegetable dumplings are everyone's favorite go-to meal. They're full of stuffing and good taste. There's a strong taste of mushrooms and cabbage in its filling.

Ingredients (6 servings)
12 Dumpling wrappers

Filling
3 tablespoons oil
1 tablespoon ginger, minced
1 large onion, chopped
2 cups shiitake mushrooms, chopped
1 ½ cups cabbage, shredded
1 ½ cups carrot, shredded
1 cup garlic chives, chopped
½ teaspoon white pepper
2 teaspoons sesame oil
3 tablespoons Shaoxing wine
2 tablespoon soy sauce
1 teaspoon sugar
Salt, to taste

Preparation

Sauté the onion with oil in a cooking pan until soft. Stir in the ginger, mushrooms, cabbage, garlic, and the rest of the ingredients. Sauté for about 7-10 minutes until the veggies are cooked and soft. Allow the filling to cool and spread the dumpling wrappers on the working surface. Divide the mushroom filling at the center of each dumpling wrapper. Wet the edges of the dumplings and bring all the edges of each dumpling together. Pinch and seal the edges of the dumplings to seal the filling inside. Boil the water in a suitable pot with a steamer basket placed inside. Add the dumplings to the steamer, cover, and steam for 20 minutes. Meanwhile, heat about 2 tablespoons of oil in a skillet. Sear for 2 minutes until golden. Serve warm.

Shrimp Dumplings

Preparation time: 10 minutes
Cook time: 20 minutes
Nutrition facts (per serving): 271 Cal (17g fat, 16g protein, 2g fiber)

If you haven't tried the famous shrimp dumplings yet, then here comes a simple and easy to cook recipe that you can recreate at home in no time with minimum efforts.

Ingredients (6 servings)

½-lb. raw shrimp, peeled, deveined

1 teaspoon oyster sauce

1 tablespoon vegetable oil

¼ teaspoon white pepper

1 teaspoon sesame oil

¼ teaspoon salt

1 teaspoon sugar

½ teaspoon ginger, minced

¼ cup bamboo shoots, chopped

12 dumpling wrappers

Preparation

Blend the shrimp with all the filling ingredients, except bamboo shoots, in a blender. Add the bamboo shoots to the blended filling and mix well. Cover and refrigerate this filling for 1 hour. Meanwhile, spread the dumpling wrappers on the working surface. Divide the shrimp filling at the center of each dumpling wrapper. Wet the edges of the dumplings and bring all the edges of each dumpling together. Pinch and seal the edges of the dumplings to seal the filling inside. Boil water in a suitable pot with a steamer basket placed inside. Add the dumplings to the steamer, cover, and steam for 6 minutes. Next, heat about 2 tablespoons of oil in a skillet. Sear the dumpling for 2 minutes until golden. Serve warm.

Chicken Potstickers

Preparation time: 10 minutes
Cook time: 24 minutes
Nutrition facts (per serving): 244 Cal (12g fat, 15g protein, 1g fiber)

These chicken potstickers have a delightful mix of cheese and chicken inside. Serve with chili sauce.

Ingredients (12 servings)

4 tablespoons oil
1 medium onion, chopped
2 stalks celery, chopped
1lb. ground chicken
½ cup hot sauce
2 cups cheddar cheese, shredded
Salt and black pepper, to taste
48 dumpling wrappers

Preparation

Sauté the onion and celery with oil in a cooking pan until soft. Stir in the chicken and cook until golden brown. Add the hot sauce, cheddar cheese, black pepper, and salt. Mix well and cook this filling for 5 minutes. Allow the filling to cool and spread the dumpling wrappers on the working surface. Divide the chicken filling at the center of each dumpling wrapper. Wet the edges of the dumplings and bring all the edges of each dumpling together. Pinch and seal the edges of the dumplings to seal the filling inside. Boil water in a suitable pot with a steamer basket placed inside. Add the dumplings to the steamer, cover and steam for 8 minutes. Meanwhile, heat about 2 tablespoons of oil in a skillet. Sear for 2 minutes until golden. Serve warm.

Chicken Mushrooms Dumplings

Preparation time: 15 minutes
Cook time: 26 minutes
Nutrition facts (per serving): 144 Cal (17g fat, 16g protein, 1g fiber)

The chicken mushrooms dumplings are here to make your dinner menu a little more delicious and nourishing.

Ingredients (12 servings)
48 dumpling wrappers
2 tablespoons vegetable oil
1 small onion, chopped
4 oz. shiitake mushrooms, chopped
6 dried shiitake mushrooms, chopped
1-lb. ground chicken
2 teaspoons sesame oil
3 tablespoons soy sauce
1 teaspoon sugar
2 tablespoons Shaoxing wine

Preparation
Sauté the onion with oil in a cooking pan until soft. Stir in the mushrooms, chicken, and the rest of the ingredients. Sauté for about 7 minutes until the veggies are cooked and soft. Allow the filling to cool and spread the dumpling wrappers on the working surface. Divide the chicken filling at the center of each dumpling wrapper. Wet the edges of the dumplings and bring all the edges of each dumpling together. Pinch and seal the edges of the dumplings to seal the filling inside. Boil water in a suitable pot with a steamer basket placed inside.

Add the dumplings to the steamer, cover and steam for 10 minutes. Meanwhile, heat about 2 tablespoons of oil in a skillet. Sear for 2 minutes until golden. Serve warm.

Gyoza Dumplings

Preparation time: 15 minutes
Cook time: 35 minutes
Nutrition facts (per serving): 226 Cal (3g fat, 13g protein, 0.1g fiber)

The appetizing and savory gyoza dumplings make a great addition to your Chinese menu, and they look great when served at the table.

Ingredients (12 servings)

5 cups Napa cabbage

8 oz. ground pork

1 garlic clove, smashed

1 ½ teaspoon fresh ginger, minced

1 scallion, chopped

2 tablespoons vegetable oil

½ teaspoon sesame oil

2 teaspoons soy sauce

¾ teaspoon sugar

½ teaspoon salt

⅛ teaspoons white pepper

24 store-bought gyoza wrappers

Preparation

Sauté the garlic, ginger, and scallions with oil in a cooking pan until soft. Stir in the cabbage, pork, and the rest of the ingredients. Sauté for about 7 minutes until veggies are cooked and soft. Allow the filling to cool and spread the gyoza wrappers on the working surface. Divide the pork filling at the center of each gyoza wrapper. Wet the edges of the dumplings and bring all the edges of each wrapper together. Pinch and seal the edges of the dumplings to seal the filling inside. Boil water in a suitable pot with a steamer basket placed inside. Add the dumplings to the steamer, cover, and steam for 20 minutes. Meanwhile, heat about 2 tablespoons of oil in a skillet. Sear the dumpling for 2 minutes until golden. Serve warm.

Zucchini Dumplings

Preparation time: 10 minutes

Cook time: 33 minutes

Nutrition facts (per serving): 123 Cal (5g fat, 4g protein, 1g fiber)

Here comes a nutri-rich meal made from all healthy ingredients- the zucchini dumplings. Serve them with a salad.

Ingredients (12 servings)

1 medium zucchini, shredded

2 ½ tablespoons vegetable oil

1 tablespoon ginger, minced

½-lb. ground chicken

¼ teaspoon white pepper

½ teaspoon sugar

1 teaspoon sesame oil

1 ½ tablespoons soy sauce

1 tablespoon Shaoxing wine

1 package dumpling wrappers

Preparation

Sauté the ginger and zucchini with oil in a cooking pan until soft. Stir in the chicken, soy sauce, and the rest of the ingredients. Sauté for about 5 minutes until the chicken is cooked and golden. Allow the filling to cool and spread the dumpling wrappers on the working surface. Divide the chicken filling at the center of each dumpling wrapper. Wet the edges of the dumplings and bring all the edges of each wrapper together. Pinch and seal the edges of the dumplings to seal the filling inside. Boil water in a suitable pot with a steamer basket placed inside. Add the dumplings to the steamer, cover, and steam for 20 minutes. Meanwhile, heat about 2 tablespoons of oil in a skillet. Sear for 2 minutes until golden. Serve warm.

Fried Spring Rolls

Preparation time: 10 minutes
Cook time: 65 minutes
Nutrition facts (per serving): 253 Cal (18g g fat, 9g protein, 3g fiber)

The famous fried spring rolls are great to serve as a side meal. Try making them at home with these healthy ingredients and enjoy.

Ingredients (12 servings)

1 ⅔ oz. dried mung bean noodles

1-lb. ground pork

2 medium carrots, grated

⅓ cup rehydrated ear mushrooms, chopped

¼ cup shallots, chopped

1 garlic clove, minced

1 teaspoon ginger, grated

1 egg white

1 tablespoon fish sauce

1 tablespoon vegetable oil

½ teaspoon salt

¼ teaspoon ground white pepper

1 cup of warm water

20 dried rice paper wrappers

Canola or vegetable oil for frying

Preparation

Soak the noodles in boiling water for 30 minutes and then drain. Sauté the carrots, shallots, and mushrooms with oil in a cooking pan until soft. Stir in the pork and the rest of the ingredients. Sauté for about 7 minutes until veggies are cooked and soft. Allow the filling to cool and spread the rice paper wrappers on the working surface. Divide the pork filling at the center of each wrapper. Wet the edges of the dumplings and bring all the edges of each wrapper together. Pinch and seal the edges of the dumplings to seal the filling inside. Boil water in a suitable pot with a steamer basket placed inside. Add the dumplings to the steamer, cover, and steam for 20 minutes. Meanwhile, heat about 2 tablespoons of oil in a skillet. Sear the dumpling for 2 minutes until golden. Serve warm.

Pork Egg Rolls

Preparation time: 10 minutes
Cook time: 20 minutes
Nutrition facts (per serving): 243 Cal (13g fat, 24g protein, 0.2g fiber)

These egg rolls are a Chinese specialty, and they're served on all special occasions. They're prepared using a nice mix of cabbage, carrot, and pork.

Ingredients (12 servings)

8 cups savoy cabbage, shredded

8 cups green cabbage, shredded

2 cups carrot, shredded

2 cups celery, shredded

3 scallions, chopped

2 ½ teaspoon salt

2 teaspoons sugar

1 tablespoon sesame oil

2 tablespoons peanut oil

¼ teaspoon five-spice powder

¼ teaspoon white pepper

3 cups roast pork minced

2 cups cooked shrimp, chopped

1 package egg roll wrappers

Preparation

Sauté the scallions, cabbage, carrot, and celery with oil in a cooking pan until soft. Stir in the pork, shrimp, and the rest of the ingredients. Sauté for about 7 minutes until the chicken is cooked and golden. Allow the filling to cool and spread the egg roll wrappers on the working surface. Divide the pork filling at the center of each wrapper. Wet the edges of the wrapper, fold the two sides, and then roll the wrappers into an egg roll. Add oil to a deep wok to 325 degrees F and then deep fry the egg rolls until golden brown. Transfer the golden egg rolls to a plate lined with a paper towel. Serve warm.

Shanghai Spring Rolls

Preparation time: 10 minutes

Cook time: 20 minutes

Nutrition facts (per serving): 252 Cal (11g fat, 17g protein, 5g fiber)

The shanghai spring rolls are one delicious way to complete your Chinese menu; here's a recipe that you can try to have a delicious meal.

Ingredients (12 servings)

⅔ cup shredded lean pork

1 small Napa cabbage, shredded

8 dried shiitake mushrooms, soaked

4 tablespoons oil

Salt, to taste

White pepper, to taste

2 tablespoons Shaoxing wine

½ teaspoon soy sauce

1 ½ tablespoon cornstarch

1 tablespoon water

2 teaspoons sesame oil

24 roll wrappers

Oil, for frying

Preparation

Mix the pork, cabbage, mushrooms, and the rest of the ingredients in a bowl, except for the roll wrappers. Sauté the filling in a suitable wok for about 10 minutes. Allow the filling to cool and spread the egg roll wrappers on the working surface. Divide the pork filling at the center of each wrapper. Wet the edges of the wrapper, fold the two sides, and then roll the wrappers into an egg roll. Add oil to a deep wok to 325 degrees F, then deep fry the egg rolls until golden brown. Transfer the golden egg rolls to a plate lined with a paper towel. Serve warm.

Chicken Phyllo Rolls

Preparation time: 10 minutes
Cook time: 13 minutes
Nutrition facts (per serving): 207 Cal (8g fat, 13g protein, 1g fiber)

This tangy tomatillo salad makes a great side serving for the table, and you can pair it with delicious and healthy entrees as well.

Ingredients (8 servings)

2 tablespoons olive oil

1 small onion, sliced

2 scallions, chopped

3 garlic cloves, minced

2 teaspoons curry powder

2 cups cooked chicken, shredded

1 tablespoon cilantro, chopped

1 lime, zested

2 tablespoons lime juice

Salt, to taste

Black pepper, to taste

4 tablespoons butter, melted

8 sheets phyllo dough

¼ cup panko breadcrumbs

Preparation

Sauté the onion, scallions, and garlic with oil in a cooking pan until soft. Stir in the chicken and the rest of the ingredients except the phyllo dough. Sauté for about 1 minute, then remove the filling from the heat. Spread a sheet of dough phyllo in a baking pan and brush it with butter. Drizzle breadcrumbs on top and repeat the layers with three more phyllo sheets. Top the four phyllo sheets with ½ of the chicken filling. Roll the sheets to make a phyllo roll. Repeat the same steps with the remaining phyllo and filling. Place the rolls in a baking tray and brush them with butter. Bake the phyllo rolls for 12 minutes in the oven at 375 degrees F. Slice and serve warm.

Cream Cheese Wontons

Preparation time: 10 minutes

Cook time: 20 minutes

Nutrition facts (per serving): 280 Cal (15g fat, 12g protein, 2g fiber)

These cream cheese wontons are made primarily from cream cheese filling, so they're easy to create. Serve them with your favorite sauce.

Ingredients (8 servings)

8 oz. cream cheese

2 teaspoons sugar

½ teaspoon salt

4 scallions, chopped

1 pack wonton wrappers

Vegetable oil for frying

Preparation

Mix the cream cheese with sugar, salt, and scallions in a bowl. Spread the egg roll wrappers on the working surface. Divide the cream cheese filling at the center of each wrapper. Wet the edges of the wrapper, fold the two sides, and then roll the wrappers into an egg roll. Add oil to a deep wok to 325 degrees F and then deep fry the egg rolls until golden brown. Transfer the golden egg rolls to a plate lined with a paper towel. Serve warm.

Soups

Hot and Sour Soup

Preparation time: 10 minutes

Cook time: 11 minutes

Nutrition facts (per serving): 336 Cal (8g fat, 32g protein, 1g fiber)

If you haven't tried the classic Chinese hot and sour soup before, then here comes a simple and easy to cook recipe that you can recreate at home in no time with minimum efforts.

Ingredients (4 servings)

½ cup lily flowers

⅓ oz. dried wood ear mushrooms, soaked

⅔ oz. dried shiitake mushrooms, soaked

3 oz. spiced dry tofu, soaked

4 oz. fresh firm tofu

7 cups vegetable stock

½ teaspoon salt

¼ teaspoon sugar

2 dried red chili peppers, chopped

2 teaspoons ground white pepper

1 ½ teaspoon mushroom dark soy sauce

1 tablespoon light soy sauce

1 teaspoon sesame oil

⅓ cup white vinegar

5 oz. bamboo shoots

¼ cup cornstarch

¼ cup water

1 large egg, beaten

1 scallion, chopped

Preparation

Sauté all the veggies and tofu with cooking in a deep soup pan until golden. Pour in the spices, sauces, vinegar, sugar, stock, and lily flowers. Cook the soup for 10 minutes on a simmer. Stir in the cornstarch slurry and then cook until it thickens. Slowly pour in the egg and cook for 1 minute with a stir. Serve warm.

Pho Noodle Soup

Preparation time: 15 minutes
Cook time: 53 minutes
Nutrition facts (per serving): 361 Cal (22g fat, 34 protein, 2g fiber)

This pho noodle soup is a must on this Chinese menu. It has a delicious mix of beef marrow, beef chuck, and fish sauce.

Ingredients (4 servings)

2 (3-inch) pieces ginger, cut in half lengthwise

2 onions, peeled

5 lbs. beef marrow

2 lbs. beef chuck, cut into 2 pieces

2 scallions, cut into 4-inch lengths

⅓ cup fish sauce

2 ½ oz. rock sugar

8-star anise

6 cloves

1 cinnamon stick

1 black cardamom pod

2 teaspoons fennel seeds

2 teaspoons coriander seeds

1 tablespoon salt

1-lb. dried pho noodles, boiled

⅓-lb. beef sirloin, sliced

Preparation

Sauté the onions and ginger with oil in a cooking pot for 5 minutes. Stir in meat and beef marrow and then cover to cook for 40 minutes. Toast all the whole spices in a dry skillet for 3 minutes and seal the spices in a spice infuser. Place the spice infuser into the broth and cover to cook for 4 hours. Stir in the sugar, salt, and fish sauce and then mix well. Remove the spice infuser from the soup. Add the remaining ingredients, including the noodles, and then cook for 5 minutes. Serve warm.

Zha Cai Noodle Soup

Preparation time: 15 minutes
Cook time: 21 minutes
Nutrition facts (per serving): 381 Cal (3 g fat, 25 g protein, 2.8g fiber)

Yes, you can make something as delicious as this Zha Cai noodle soup by using some popular Chinese ingredients like Shaoxing wine, white noodles, and pork.

Ingredients (4 servings)
Pork
4-6 oz. pork shoulder, cut into thin strips
1 teaspoon cornstarch
1 teaspoon vegetable oil
1 teaspoon Shaoxing wine
1 teaspoon oyster sauce
⅛ teaspoon salt

Soup
8 oz. fresh white noodles, cooked
4 cups chicken stock
1 tablespoon vegetable oil
7 oz. pickled mustard stems
¼ teaspoon sugar
½ teaspoon sesame oil
1 scallion, chopped

Preparation

Mix the cornstarch with wine, oyster sauce, and salt in a bowl. Stir in the pork slices and mix well. Cover to marinate for 10 minutes. Add oil and marinated pork to a skillet and then sear them until golden brown. Transfer this brown pork to a plate and keep it aside. Sauté the mustard stems and scallions with sesame and vegetable oil in a soup pot for 1 minute. Stir in the stock, sugar, pork, and noodles. Cook the pork soup for 10 minutes. Serve warm.

Chongqing Noodle Soup

Preparation time: 15 minutes
Cook time: 20 minutes
Nutrition facts (per serving): 381 Cal (6g fat, 24g protein, 0.6g fiber)

The Chinese Chongqing Noodle soup has no parallel in taste. It has a unique blend of sweet potato noodles, soybeans, and a mix of soy sauce.

Ingredients (4 servings)

3 tablespoons roasted soybeans

3 ½ oz. dried sweet potato noodles

2 ½ cups stock

1 ginger slice, minced

2 garlic cloves, minced

1 teaspoon toasted sesame seeds

1 teaspoon Sichuan chili flakes

2 tablespoons vegetable oil

2 tablespoons Chinese black vinegar

2 tablespoons light soy sauce

½ teaspoon dark soy sauce

½ teaspoon sugar

½ teaspoon Sichuan peppercorn powder

¼ teaspoon white pepper

½ teaspoon sesame oil

1 tablespoon chili oil

¼ cup pickled mustard stems

1 scallion, chopped

1 tablespoon cilantro, chopped

Preparation

Sauté the soybeans, scallion, ginger, garlic, and mustard stem with oil in a soup pan for 5 minutes. Stir in the stock and all other ingredients and cover to cook for 15 minutes. Serve warm.

Chicken Noodle Wonton Soup

Preparation time: 15 minutes

Cook time: 17 minutes

Nutrition facts (per serving): 248 Cal (8g fat, 22g protein, 1g fiber)

A perfect mix of beef, beans, chipotle with chicken, noodles, and wonton in a single soup is all that you need to expand your Chinese menu. Simple and easy to make, this recipe is a must to try.

Ingredients (4 servings)

Wontons

1-lb. ground chicken

½ cup parsley, chopped

1 garlic clove

¼ cup water

2 tablespoons dry sherry

Juice of ½ a lemon

1 tablespoon oil

1 teaspoon salt

1 teaspoon sugar

½ teaspoon dried thyme

½ teaspoon black pepper

2 tablespoons butter, melted

1 package wonton wrappers

Soup

1 tablespoon oil

½ white onion, diced

3 medium carrots, diced

3 stalks celery, diced

5 cups chicken broth

Salt and black pepper, to taste

Preparation

Mix the chicken, oil, salt, sugar, thyme, garlic, ginger, black pepper, parsley, lemon juice, and sherry in a bowl. Spread the wonton wrappers on the working surface. Divide the filling on top of the wrappers and wet the edges. Fold the wrappers in half and seal the two edges of the wontons. Sauté the onion, carrot, and celery with oil in a soup pan for 5 minutes. Pour in the stock, black pepper, salt, and prepared wontons. Cover and cook the soup for 12 minutes on medium heat. Serve warm.

Tomato Egg Drop Soup

Preparation time: 10 minutes
Cook time: 11 minutes
Nutrition facts (per serving): 368 Cal (21g fat, 28g protein, 1g fiber)

Serve the warming bowl of tomato egg drop soup and make your meal a little more nutritional. It has everything healthy in it, ranging from tomatoes, eggs, and spices.

Ingredients (4 servings)

2 tablespoons oil

10 oz. tomatoes, diced

1 cup chicken stock

2 cups of water

2 teaspoons soy sauce

½ teaspoon sesame oil

¼ teaspoon white pepper

Salt, to taste

1 egg, beaten

1 ½ teaspoon cornstarch

2 tablespoons water

1 scallion, chopped

2 tablespoons cilantro, chopped

Preparation

Sauté the tomatoes with oil in a soup pan for 5 minutes. Stir in the stock, water, soy sauce, sesame oil, white pepper, and salt and then cook for 5 minutes. Pour in the cornstarch slurry and then cook until the soup thickens. Stir in the egg and cook for 1 minute. Garnish with scallion and cilantro. Enjoy.

Chinese Winter Melon Soup

Preparation time: 5 minutes
Cook time: 13 minutes
Nutrition facts (per serving): 345 Cal (21g fat, 26g protein, 2g fiber)

This Chinese winter melon soup is a typical Chinese entree, which is a staple on a healthy menu. It has this rich mix of pork meatballs with glass noodles and winter melon.

Ingredients (6 servings)
Meatballs
1-lb. ground pork

2 tablespoons water

2 ½ tablespoon light soy sauce

2 tablespoons Shaoxing wine

1 teaspoon sesame oil

½ teaspoon ground white pepper

½ teaspoon sugar

1 egg white

1 tablespoon ginger, minced

1 scallion, chopped

¼ teaspoon salt

Soup
1 package glass noodles, boiled

1-lb. winter melon, peeled and diced

1 tablespoon oil

2 scallions, chopped

4 cups chicken stock

2 cups of water

½ teaspoon ground white pepper

½ teaspoon sesame oil

Salt, to taste

1 handful of cilantro, chopped

Preparation

Mix the pork with water, soy sauce, wine, sesame oil, white pepper, sugar, egg white, ginger, scallions, and salt in a bowl. Make small meatballs from this pork mixture. Sauté the meatballs with 1 tablespoon oil in a soup pot until golden brown. Stir in the scallions and melon and then sauté for 2 minutes. Add the remaining soup ingredients along with the boiled noodles. Cook the soup for 10 minutes on medium heat until the meatballs are done. Serve warm.

Cantonese Pork Soup

Preparation time: 10 minutes

Cook time: 3 hours

Nutrition facts (per serving): 430 Cal (29g fat, 27g protein, 3g fiber)

Try this Chinese pork soup with your favorite herbs on top. Adding a dollop of cream or yogurt will make it even richer in taste.

Ingredients (8 servings)

4 dried shiitake mushrooms, soaked and drained

1 ⅓ lbs. lean pork shoulder

1-lb. large carrots, cut into chunks

2 tablespoons dried red dates, pitted and halved

2 tablespoons dried goji berries

1 large chunk ginger, smashed

14 cups water

1-lb. Chinese yams, peeled and cut into chunks

Salt, to taste

Preparation

Add the pork, mushrooms, carrots, red dates, goji berries, ginger, water, and salt to a soup pot. Cover and cook for 2 hours on a simmer and then add the Chinese yam. Cook for another 1 hour on a simmer. Serve warm.

Chinese Rice Cake Soup

Preparation time: 10 minutes
Cook time: 35 minutes
Nutrition facts (per serving): 225 Cal (4g fat, 14g protein, 3g fiber)

Enjoy this Chinese rice cake soup with crispy bread and a fresh vegetable salad on the side. The warming bowl of this soup makes a great serving for all the special dinners.

Ingredients (4 servings)
Meat
½-lb. lean pork, cut into strips
2 teaspoons Shaoxing wine
1 tablespoon light soy sauce
½ teaspoon sesame oil
¼ teaspoon white pepper
2 teaspoons cornstarch
1 teaspoon water

Soup
4 tablespoons vegetable oil
4 ginger slices, julienned
3 scallions, sliced
1 small carrot, sliced
1 ¼ lbs. Napa cabbage, diced
4 cups chicken stock
4 cups of water
½ teaspoon white pepper

1 teaspoon sesame oil

1 tablespoon light soy sauce

1-lb. rice cakes, oval-shaped slices

Preparation

Mix the pork with soy sauce, sesame oil, water, cornstarch, white pepper, and wine in a bowl. Cover the pork and marinate for 20 minutes. Sauté the pork with the remaining oil in a soup pot until brown. Stir in the ginger and the rest of the ingredients and then sauté for 4 minutes. Pour in the water, stock, white pepper, and soy sauce and cook the soup for 10 minutes. Add the rice cakes and cook for 1 minute on medium heat. Serve warm.

Laksa Noodle Soup

Preparation time: 15 minutes
Cook time: 62 minutes
Nutrition facts (per serving): 401 Cal (20g fat, 36g protein, 4g fiber)

You cannot expect to have Chinese cuisine and not try the traditional laksa noodle soup in it. This chicken soup is full of chilies and coconut milk.

Ingredients (4 servings)
4 bone-in chicken thighs
4 tablespoons vegetable oil
1 garlic clove, minced
1 ½ tablespoon ginger, minced
1 stalk lemongrass, minced
2 Thai chilies, minced
½ cup laksa paste
1 tablespoon brown sugar
4 cups chicken stock
1 can coconut milk
1 tablespoon fish sauce
1 package soy puffs, halved
4 portions of noodles
1-3 limes, juices
3 large shallots, sliced
¼ cup all-purpose flour
12 large shrimp
2 cups mung bean sprouts
½ cup fresh cilantro leaves

Preparation

Season the chicken thighs with black pepper and salt. Place them on a baking tray and bake for 40 minutes at 400 degrees F. Meanwhile, sauté the ginger and garlic with 2 tablespoons oil for 1 minute in a saucepan. Stir in the chilies and lemongrass and then sauté for 3 minutes. Add the brown sugar and the laksa paste and then cook for 3 minutes. Stir in the fish sauce, coconut milk, and chicken stock and then cook this mixture to a boil. Add the soy puffs, cover the soup, and cook for 10 minutes on a simmer. Cook the noodles in boiling water according to the package's instructions. Add the noodles, along with the remaining ingredients, to the soup. Cook for 5 minutes and then serve warm.

Cantonese Chicken Feet Soup

Preparation time: 15 minutes
Cook time: 2 hours 20 minutes
Nutrition facts (per serving): 490 Cal (22g fat, 27g protein, 2g fiber)

Loaded with lots of flavors, this Cantonese chicken feet soup makes an amazing serving for all your meals. Enjoy it warm with your favorite bread.

Ingredients (8 servings)

2 tablespoons dried seaweed, soaked
1 cup raw shelled peanuts
1 ½ lbs. chicken feet
2 tablespoons Shaoxing wine
4 ginger slices
12 cups water
Salt, to taste
1 scallion, chopped

Preparation

Add water, ginger, wine, chicken feet, seaweed, peanuts, and salt in a large soup pot. Cook the chicken feet soup for 20 minutes and reduce the heat to low. Continue cooking for 2 hours and then garnish with scallions. Serve warm.

Matzo Ball Soup

Preparation time: 10 minutes
Cook time: 1 hour 20 minutes
Nutrition facts (per serving): 267 Cal (6g fat, 10g protein, 1.2g fiber)

Try this super tasty Chinese matzo ball soup prepared with matzo meal, carrots, and celery. Make your meals special, and you'll never stop having it; that's how heavenly the combination tastes.

Ingredients (4 servings)

1 cup matzo meal
¼ cup of vegetable oil
¼ cup chicken stock
4 large eggs
¼ teaspoon nutmeg
½ teaspoon baking powder

Soup

Salt and black pepper, to taste
6 cups chicken stock
4 ribs celery, diced
3 medium carrots, diced
1 small onion, diced

Preparation

Mix matzo meal with eggs, salt, black pepper, nutmeg, vegetable oil, baking powder, and stock in a bowl. Cover and refrigerate this mixture for 3 hours. Add the chicken stock, onion, carrots and celery in a soup pot. Cook the soup for 40 minutes on low heat until the veggies are soft. Meanwhile, set a pot filled with salted water. Make small balls from the matzo mixture. Add the matzo balls to the water and cook for 35 minutes. Transfer the matzo balls to the soup and cook for 5 minutes. Serve warm.

Shepherd's Tofu Soup

Preparation time: 10 minutes

Cook time: 20 minutes

Nutrition facts (per serving): 238 Cal (2g fat, 31g protein, 1g fiber)

If you haven't tried the shepherd's tofu soup before, then here comes a simple and easy cook recipe that you can recreate at home in no time with minimum effort.

Ingredients (4 servings)

8 oz. frozen Shepherd's purse or frozen spinach

½ block silken tofu

4 cups chicken stock

1 ½ teaspoon salt

1 teaspoon sesame oil

¼ teaspoon ground white pepper

¼ cup cornstarch

¼ cup of water

3 egg whites

Preparation

Sauté the tofu and the shepherd's purse with sesame oil in a soup pot for 5 minutes. Stir in the stock, salt, and white pepper and t cook this mixture on a simmer for 10 minutes. Mix the corn-starch with water and pour into the soup. Cook the soup until it thickens. Beat the egg whites and pour them into the soup. Cook for 5 minutes and then serve warm.

Seaweed Egg Drop Soup

Preparation time: 15 minutes
Cook time: 10 minutes
Nutrition facts (per serving): 357 Cal (5g fat, 21g protein, 0g fiber)

This seaweed egg drop soup is a healthy entrée that can be served with a tasty salad on the side, which will enhance its flavor and will make it more nutritious.

Ingredients (4 servings)

2 tablespoons dried seaweed
4 cups chicken stock
1 cup of water
5 g dried shrimp flakes
¼-½ teaspoon sesame oil
¼ teaspoon white pepper
2 eggs, beaten
1 scallion, sliced

Preparation

Sauté the seaweed in a suitable wok for 2 minutes and then add water and chicken stock. Boil the stock, and add the shrimp flakes, sesame oil, seaweed, and white pepper. Cook the mixture to a boil and then stir in the eggs and scallions. Serve warm.

Main Dishes

Sweet and Sour Fish

Preparation time: 15 minutes

Cook time: 20 minutes

Nutrition facts (per serving): 365 Cal (17g fat, 32g protein, 10g fiber)

You can give this sweet and sour fish a try because it has a good and delicious combination of cod fillet and a savory sour sauce.

Ingredients (2 servings)

Fish

12 oz. cod fillet, cut into cubes

3 cups canola oil, for frying

¾ cup all-purpose flour

¼ teaspoon baking powder

1 tablespoon cornstarch

½ teaspoon salt

⅛ teaspoon turmeric powder

⅛ teaspoon white pepper

¼ teaspoon sesame oil

⅔ cup cold seltzer or club soda

Sweet and sour sauce

¼ cup red onion, diced

¼ cup red bell peppers, diced

¼ cup green bell peppers, diced

1 tablespoon ketchup

¾ cup canned pineapple chunks

¾ cup pineapple juice

2 ½ tablespoons red wine vinegar

⅓ cup of water

¼ teaspoon salt

2 tablespoons sugar

1 ½ tablespoon cornstarch

Preparation

Mix the cornstarch, flour, salt, turmeric, white pepper, sesame oil, club soda, and baking powder in a bowl. Dip the fillets in the soda-flour mixture to coat well. Add 3 cups oil to a deep pan and heat to 350 degrees F. Deep fry the fish fillets until golden brown. Transfer the fillets to a plate lined with a paper towel and then cover with a foil sheet. Sauté the onion and peppers with oil in a cooking pan for 30 seconds. Stir in the ketchup and sauté for 20 seconds. Stir in the sugar, salt, vinegar, pineapple, and pineapple juices. Cook this sauce for 2 minutes on a low simmer. Stir in the cornstarch, mix gently, and cook until it makes a thick sauce. Pour this sauce over the fillets. Serve warm.

Fried Flounder

Preparation time: 15 minutes
Cook time: 20 minutes
Nutrition facts (per serving): 381 Cal (6g fat, 23g protein, 1g fiber)

If you're bored with the usual seafood recipe, then this Chinese flounder recipe is one unique option. Enjoy it with fried rice and noodles on the side.

Ingredients (2 servings)

1-1¼ lbs. whole flounder, sole, or fluke

2 teaspoons Shaoxing wine

¾ teaspoon salt

½ teaspoon white pepper

3 tablespoons cornstarch

⅔ cup canola oil

Sauce

1½ tablespoons hot water

¼ teaspoon sugar

1½ tablespoons soy sauce

2 teaspoons Shaoxing wine

3 tablespoons oil

1 scallion, julienned

1 small handful cilantro, chopped

Preparation

Mix the hot water, sugar, soy sauce, wine, scallion, cilantro, and oil in a saucepan. Cook this mixture for 5 minutes with occasional stirring, and then allow the sauce to cool. Mix the cornstarch with white pepper, salt, and wine in a bowl. Coat the flounder with the cornstarch mixture. Heat the oil in a deep pan for deep frying and deep fry the flounder until golden brown. Transfer the flounder to a plate lined with a paper towel. Pour the prepared sauce over the fillet. Serve warm.

Shanghai Smoked Fish

Preparation time: 15 minutes
Cook time: 20 minutes
Nutrition facts (per serving): 395 Cal (11g fat, 24g protein, 1g fiber)

The delicious shanghai smoked fish will satisfy your seafood cravings in no time. It's quick to make at home.

Ingredients (4 servings)
Fish and marinade
2½ lbs. small buffalo carp, cut into ¾-inch thick sections
4 tablespoons Shaoxing wine
½ teaspoon ground white pepper
½ teaspoon salt
3 teaspoons ginger, grated

Sauce
3 cups of water
4 ginger slices
2-star anise
1 cinnamon stick
5 bay leaves
⅔ oz. brown rock sugar
½ cup Shaoxing wine
1 tablespoon oyster sauce
5 tablespoons light soy sauce
1½ tablespoons dark soy sauce
½ teaspoon Chinese black vinegar

4 scallions

½ cup of orange juice

Preparation

Mix the wine with white pepper, salt, and ginger in a large shallow bowl. Add the fish fillets to the wine mixture and cover to marinate for 24 hours in the refrigerator. Prepare the sauce, add water, ginger, star anise, cinnamon, bay leaves, brown sugar, wine, soy sauce, black vinegar, scallions, and orange juice in a saucepan. Cook this mixture on medium heat until the sauce is reduced to half. Strain the mixture and allow it to cool. Meanwhile, remove the fish from the marinade and keep it aside. Heat the oil in a deep pan for deep frying and fry the fish until golden brown. Transfer the fish to a plate lined with a paper towel. Pour the prepared sauce on top. Serve warm.

Shrimp Stir-Fry

Preparation time: 15 minutes
Cook time: 15 minutes
Nutrition facts (per serving): 379 Cal (11g fat, 26g protein, 6g fiber)

This shrimp stir fry is known as a classic Chinese entrée. The fried shrimp with sauces makes a great serving for the table.

Ingredients (4 servings)
12 oz. large, shell-on headless shrimp
2 tablespoons vegetable oil
7 fresh ginger slices, cut ⅛-inch thick
1 garlic clove, sliced
2 scallions, chopped
¼ cup ketchup
1 teaspoon Worcestershire sauce
⅛ teaspoon white pepper
½ teaspoon sugar
2 tablespoons Shaoxing wine
1 tablespoon soy sauce

Preparation
Mix the ketchup, Worcestershire sauce, white pepper, sugar, wine, soy sauce, scallions, garlic, and ginger in a cooking pan. Cook the sauce for 5 minutes on medium heat, and then remove it from the heat. Sauté the shrimp with 1 tablespoon canola oil in a suitable wok until they turn golden brown in color. Pour in the sauce and toss gently to coat the shrimp. Serve warm.

Hunan Fish

Preparation time: 5 minutes

Cook time: 10 minutes

Nutrition facts (per serving): 206 Cal (15g fat, 21g protein, 1g fiber)

Try the Chinese Hunan style tilapia fish and cook it quickly to serve at your dinner table. Pair this dish with sautéed asparagus and mushrooms.

Ingredients (4 servings)

1 ½ lbs. fresh tilapia

16 oz. silken tofu

⅛ teaspoon salt

3 tablespoons canola oil

1 ½ tablespoons ginger, minced

6 tablespoons Duo Jiao

3 garlic cloves, minced

1 scallion, diced

⅔ cup hot water

2 tablespoons soy sauce

1 teaspoon sugar

¼ teaspoon white pepper

Preparation

Mix hot water, soy sauce, sugar, white pepper, garlic, ginger, salt, scallions, and Duo Jiao in a saucepan. Cook this sauce until the sauce is reduced to half, and then allow it to cool. Soak the tofu and fillets in the prepared sauce, rub well, and cover to marinate for 30 minutes. Add oil to a cooking pan and place it over medium heat. Sear the tofu and fish in the skillet for 5 minutes per side until golden brown. Serve warm.

Shrimp and Broccoli

Preparation time: 15 minutes
Cook time: 15 minutes
Nutrition facts (per serving): 228 Cal (6g fat, 14g protein, 3g fiber)

Here's a famous Chinese shrimp broccoli recipe that's mostly served at the dinner table. It has a blend of rich and nutritious ingredients like shrimp, broccoli, and soy sauces.

Ingredients (4 servings)

16 shrimp, peeled, deveined, and butterflied

10 oz. broccoli florets

½ cup chicken stock

¼ teaspoon granulated sugar

1 ½ tablespoon soy sauce

½ teaspoon dark soy sauce

1 tablespoon oyster sauce

½ teaspoon sesame oil

⅛ teaspoon white pepper

2 tablespoons canola oil

2 garlic cloves, chopped

1 tablespoon Shaoxing wine

1 ½ tablespoon cornstarch

2 tablespoons water

Preparation

Add sesame oil to a large cooking pot and stir in the garlic. Sauté until the garlic turns golden and then add the broccoli. Stir and cook for 5 minutes until soft.

Add the shrimp, sugar, soy sauce, chicken stock, oyster sauce, white pepper, and wine to the saucepan. Cook the mixture until the shrimp are tender. Stir in the cornstarch, mix, and cook until the mixture thickens. Serve warm.

Typhoon Shrimp

Preparation time: 10 minutes
Cook time: 11 minutes
Nutrition facts (per serving): 303 Cal (7g fat, 33g protein, 1g fiber)

Here's a delicious shrimp meal loaded with flavors. Serve these shrimps with hot bread for the best experience.

Ingredients (4 servings)

1 lb. large, head-on shrimp

¼ teaspoon white pepper powder

2 teaspoons Shaoxing wine

4 ginger slices, minced

7 garlic cloves, minced

2 scallions, chopped

3 red chilies, chopped

1 cup panko breadcrumbs

1 cup of vegetable oil

½ teaspoon salt

¼ teaspoon sugar

⅛ teaspoon five-spice powder

Preparation

Sauté ginger and garlic with vegetable oil in a skillet until golden brown. Stir in the white pepper, wine, red chilies, scallions, salt, sugar, and spice powder. Mix and toss in the shrimp and then cook for 5-6 minutes. Spread the shrimp in a baking dish and drizzle the panko crumbs on top. Bake the shrimp for 2 minutes in the oven at 350 degrees F. Serve warm.

Pepper Tofu

Preparation time: 15 minutes
Cook time: 10 minutes
Nutrition facts (per serving): 256 Cal (22g fat, 13g protein, 18g fiber)

Have you tried the basic black pepper tofu? Well, here's a Chinese delight that adds tofu with sauces to your dinner table in a delicious way.

Ingredients (2 servings)
Tofu brine
14 oz. firm tofu, sliced
¼ teaspoon garlic powder
½ teaspoon onion powder
½ teaspoon salt
1 teaspoon sugar
1 ¼ cups warm water
½ teaspoon sesame oil
1 teaspoon Shaoxing wine

Tofu seasoning
¾ teaspoon salt
¾ teaspoon ground white pepper
¼ teaspoon ground Sichuan Peppercorn
¼ teaspoon sand ginger powder
2 tablespoons all-purpose flour
2 tablespoons cornstarch

Dish

4 tablespoons vegetable oil

5 garlic cloves, chopped

1 long hot green pepper, sliced

1 shallot, sliced

1 scallion, chopped

1 tablespoon cilantro, chopped

Preparation

Mix the tofu with all of its brine ingredients in a bowl and cover to marinate for 2 hours. Whisk flour with cornstarch, peppercorn, white pepper, salt, and ginger powder in a bowl. To cook the tofu, heat the oil in a suitable wok. Dredge the marinated tofu through the flour mixture and sear in the wok until golden from both sides. Stir in the rest of the ingredients and cook for 5 minutes. Serve warm.

Gingered Tofu

Preparation time: 10 minutes
Cook time: 25 minutes
Nutrition facts (per serving): 491 Cal (33g fat, 29g protein, 2g fiber)

This gingered tofu meal is known as the classic Chinese dinner. Enjoy this tofu with a seaweed salad or roasted asparagus on the side.

Ingredients (2 servings)
21 oz. firm tofu, cut into cubes
2 tablespoons oil
4 ginger slices
1 tablespoon Shaoxing wine
2 tablespoons Chinese black vinegar
3 tablespoons light soy sauce
4 tablespoons sugar
5 tablespoons water

Preparation
Sauté the ginger with oil in a suitable wok for 30 seconds. Stir in the tofu and sauté for 10 minutes until it turns golden. Add the wine, black vinegar, soy sauce, water, and sugar. Cover and cook for 15 minutes over medium-low heat. Serve warm.

Steamed Seitan

Preparation time: 10 minutes
Cook time: 16 minutes
Nutrition facts (per serving): 350 Cal (17g fat, 37g protein, 1.2g fiber)

Steamed seitan is another popular entrée that's known for its mixture of mushrooms with dried lily flowers and seitan.

Ingredients (4 servings)
⅓ cup dried wood ear mushrooms, soaked
½ cup dried lily flowers, soaked
4 large dried shiitake mushrooms, soaked
1 ½ cups seitan, cut into bite-sized pieces
½ cup mushroom soaking liquid
1 tablespoon vegetable oil
½ teaspoon sesame oil
1 tablespoon Shaoxing wine
1 tablespoon oyster sauce
½ teaspoon sugar
¾ teaspoon salt
¼ teaspoon white pepper
1 teaspoon ginger, grated
1 scallion, chopped
1 ½ tablespoon cornstarch

Preparation
Drain the mushrooms, lily flowers, and wood ears and transfer to a wok. Add ginger, oil, soaking liquid, oyster sauce, sugar, salt, white pepper, and the white

part of the scallions. Cook until the liquid is absorbed and then add the green parts of the scallions. Stir and cook for 30 seconds and then add the cornstarch, seitan, and the rest of the ingredients. Mix well, cover, and cook for 15 minutes on medium-low heat. Serve warm.

General Tso's Vegetables

Preparation time: 15 minutes
Cook time: 15 minutes
Nutrition facts (per serving): 360 Cal (21g fat, 21g protein, 1g fiber)

If you haven't tried the famous vegan general Tso's before, then here comes a simple and easy cook recipe that you can recreate at home in no time with minimum effort.

Ingredients (4 servings)
Sauce
⅓ cup Asian vegetable stock
1 teaspoon dark soy sauce
1 tablespoon soy sauce
2 teaspoons rice vinegar
1 teaspoon Shaoxing wine
3 ½ tablespoon brown sugar
¼ teaspoon white pepper

Dish
1-lb. cauliflower floret
2 cups broccoli florets
1 tablespoon vegetable oil
4-5 dried red chili peppers
3 garlic cloves, minced
1 tablespoon cornstarch
2 tablespoons water

Preparation

Mix all the sauce ingredients in a bowl and keep it aside. Sauté the cauliflower, broccoli, and garlic with oil in a suitable wok for 5 minutes. Pour in the sauce and add cornstarch and then mix well. Cover and cook for 10 minutes on medium-low heat. Serve warm.

Oyster Mushroom

Preparation time: 15 minutes

Cook time: 10 minutes

Nutrition facts (per serving): 275 Cal (23g fat, 15g protein, 1g fiber)

The Chinese oyster mushrooms with bean sauce sound delicious to serve at the dinner table. It's known for its comforting taste and the energizing combination of ingredients.

Ingredients (4 servings)

1 lb. king oyster mushrooms, sliced

5 tablespoons vegetable oil

6 ginger slices

8 garlic cloves, sliced

1 tablespoon spicy bean sauce

1 tablespoon light soy sauce

½ teaspoon sugar

5 long hot peppers, sliced

Preparation

Sauté the mushrooms, ginger, and garlic with oil in a suitable wok for 5 minutes. Stir in the bean sauce, soy sauce, sugar, and hot peppers. Mix well and cover to cook for 5 minutes on low heat. Serve warm.

Kung Pao Tofu

Preparation time: 10 minutes
Cook time: 10 minutes
Nutrition facts (per serving): 388 Cal (11g fat, 28g protein, 3g fiber)

This Chinese kung pao tofu is everything you must be looking for to make your dinner loaded with nutrients. The combination of tofu and sauces make a complete package for a health enthusiast like me.

Ingredients (4 servings)
Tofu
14 oz. firm tofu
⅓ cup cornstarch
¼ teaspoon garlic powder
¼ teaspoon onion powder
⅛ teaspoon five-spice powder
¼ teaspoon salt
¼ cup water

For the rest
1 tablespoon soy sauce
½ teaspoon dark soy sauce
2 teaspoons sugar
¼ teaspoon salt
1 ½ teaspoon rice vinegar
½ teaspoon sesame oil
2 teaspoons cornstarch
⅔ cup warm water

¼ cup peanut oil

1 cup blanched peanuts

2 medium carrots chopped

1 tablespoon ginger, minced

3-5 dried chili peppers, chopped

3 garlic cloves, chopped

3 scallions, diced

1 teaspoon Sichuan peppercorn powder

Preparation

For the tofu, mix the cornstarch with water, salt, 5 spice powder, onion powder, and garlic powder in a bowl. Mix the soy sauces, sugar, salt, rice vinegar, cornstarch, sesame oil, and warm water in a bowl. Sauté the peanuts with ¼ cup peanut oil in a suitable wok for 5 minutes and then transfer to a plate. Sear the tofu in the same oil until golden brown, then transfer to a plate. Now sauté the ginger and chili peppers with 1 ½ tablespoon peanut oil in a suitable wok for 1 minute. Add the tofu, peanuts, and prepared sauce. Mix well and garnish with peppercorn. Enjoy.

Braised Tofu

Preparation time: 15 minutes
Cook time: 15 minutes
Nutrition facts (per serving): 405 Cal (4g fat, 23g protein, 2g fiber)

This braised tofu is loved by all, young and adult. It's simple and quick to make. This delight is great to serve at dinner tables.

Ingredients (4 servings)

1-lb. silken tofu

2 cups oil for frying

1 cup chicken stock

1 tablespoon oyster sauce

1 ½ tablespoon soy sauce

1 teaspoon dark soy sauce

½ teaspoon sesame oil

¼ teaspoon sugar

¼ teaspoon salt

3 small ginger slices

3 garlic cloves, minced

2 scallions, chopped

4 fresh shiitake mushrooms

1 medium carrot, sliced

⅔ cup fresh winter bamboo shoots

1 tablespoon Shaoxing wine

½ cup snap peas

1 ½ tablespoon cornstarch

Preparation

In a deep pan, heat 2 cups oil and deep fry the tofu until golden brown. Transfer the tofu to a plate and keep it aside. Sauté the ginger with oil in a suitable wok for 15 seconds. Stir in the mushrooms, carrots, scallions, and bamboo shoots and cook for 30 seconds. Add the snap peas, wine, all the sauces, sesame oil, sugar, and salt and then cook for 4 minutes. Mix the cornstarch with water in a bowl and pour into the wok. Stir and cook for 1-2 minutes until the mixture thickens. Toss in the deep-fried tofu and mix well to coat. Serve warm.

Tofu with Black Bean Sauce

Preparation time: 10 minutes
Cook time: 10 minutes
Nutrition facts (per serving): 425 Cal (17g fat, 15g protein, 0.8g fiber)

Here comes the famous tofu with black bean sauce that can be served with white rice or fried rice. Add a drizzle of sesame seeds on top before serving.

Ingredients (4 servings)
1-lb. firm tofu, diced
3 tablespoons oil
2 garlic cloves, minced
2 tablespoons fermented black beans, rinsed
2 scallions, whites and greens, separated
3 dried red chilies, deseeded and chopped
1 tablespoon Shaoxing wine
½ tablespoon light soy sauce
½ teaspoon sesame oil
¼ teaspoon ground white pepper
¼ teaspoon sugar
1 teaspoon cornstarch
2 tablespoons water

Preparation
Sauté the garlic with oil in a large wok for 30 seconds. Stir in the tofu and cook it for 5 minutes until golden brown. Add the black beans, wine, soy sauce, red chilies, white pepper, and sugar. Next, cover to cook for 3 minutes. Stir in the cornstarch, mix well, and cook for 2 minutes. Garnish with scallions. Serve warm.

Beef Chow Fun

Preparation time: 15 minutes
Cook time: 15 minutes
Nutrition facts (per serving): 389 Cal (13g fat, 23g protein, 2g fiber)

If you haven't tried the famous beef chow fun before, then here comes a simple and easy to cook recipe that you can recreate at home in no time with minimum efforts.

Ingredients (4 servings)

Beef

8 oz. flank steak, sliced into ⅛ thick pieces
¼ teaspoon baking soda
1 teaspoon cornstarch
1 teaspoon soy sauce
1 teaspoon vegetable oil

Dish

12 oz. fresh wide rice noodles, boiled
3 tablespoons vegetable oil
4 scallions, cut into 3-inch pieces
3 thin ginger slices
2 tablespoons Shaoxing wine
½ teaspoon sesame oil
2 teaspoons dark soy sauce
2 tablespoons soy sauce
⅛ teaspoon sugar
Salt and white pepper, to taste
6 oz. fresh mung bean sprouts

Preparation

Season the flank steak with soya sauce, cornstarch, and baking soda. Sear the flank with vegetable oil in a skillet over medium heat until golden brown. Sauté the ginger and bean sprouts with vegetable oil in a suitable wok for 1 minute. Stir in the flank steaks, wine, sesame oil, soy sauce, sugar, and white pepper. Mix well, cook it for about 1 minute, and then toss in the noodles. Serve warm.

Fuqi Feipian

Preparation time: 15 minutes
Cook time: 50 minutes
Nutrition facts (per serving): 310 Cal (6g fat, 32g protein, 0g fiber)

It's basically a spicy beef shank and beef tripe meal, and it's known for its super-nutritious blend of ingredients. It tastes great when served with a dollop of cream or yogurt.

Ingredients (4 servings)
Meat
2 lbs. beef shank

1 ½ lbs. honeycomb beef tripe

5 ginger slices

3 scallions

2 teaspoons Sichuan peppercorns

1 teaspoon cumin seeds

1 teaspoon coriander seeds

1 teaspoon black or white peppercorns

3 cloves

3 bay leaves

1 cinnamon stick

½ dried tangerine peel

2-star anise

1 black cardamom pod

2 white cardamom pods

⅓ cup Shaoxing wine

⅓ cup light soy sauce

1 tablespoon dark soy sauce

2 tablespoons rock sugar

Sauce

¼ cup braising liquid

¼ cup chili oil

2 garlic cloves, minced

1 teaspoon Sichuan peppercorn powder

1 tablespoon toasted sesame seeds

2 teaspoons Chinese black vinegar

1 tablespoon light soy sauce

1 ½ teaspoon sugar

¼ teaspoon salt

Servings

⅓ cup Chinese celery, chopped

¼ cup roasted peanuts, chopped

2 tablespoons cilantro, chopped

Preparation

Add the tripe, ginger, and beef shank to a cooking pot and pour in water to cover them. Boil the meat for 1 minute, drain, and rinse the meat. Return the beef and tripe to a cooking pot and pour enough water to cover it. Stir in the scallions, sugar, soy sauce, and all the ingredients for the meat. Cover and cook this meat for 45 minutes on a simmer. Strain and reserve the braising liquid. Mix all the ingredients for the liquid sauce in a bowl. Slice the tripe and beef, then transfer to a serving platter. Pour the sauce and celery on top. Garnish with cilantro and peanuts. Enjoy.

Steak Stir Fry

Preparation time: 5 minutes

Cook time: 20 minutes

Nutrition facts (per serving): 423 Cal (17g fat, 23g protein, 1g fiber)

The Chinese steak stir fry is loved by all due to its amazing blend of beef and steak sauce. This meal makes an irresistible serving for the table.

Ingredients (4 servings)

Steak and marinade

1-lb. beef ribeye, cut into cubes

1 ½ tablespoon vegetable oil

⅛ teaspoon baking soda

1 teaspoon cornstarch

¼ teaspoon salt

Steak sauce

5 tablespoons water

1 teaspoon ketchup

1 teaspoon Worcestershire sauce

2 teaspoons soy sauce

2 teaspoons oyster sauce

⅛ teaspoon ground white pepper

⅛ teaspoon sesame oil

1 tablespoon cornstarch

1 tablespoon water

Bok choy

12 oz. fresh bok choy, cut and washed

1 tablespoon vegetable oil

3-4 fresh ginger slices, smashed

3 garlic cloves, chopped

½ teaspoon salt

⅛ teaspoon sugar

⅛ teaspoon MSG

Preparation

Mix the ketchup and all the ingredients for the sauce in a bowl. Coat the beef cubes with cornstarch, salt, and baking soda. Sear the beef with vegetable oil in a skillet until golden brown. Sauté the ginger, bok choy, salt, sugar, MSG, and garlic with oil in a suitable wok for 5 minutes. Add the beef cubes and the sauce into the wok and then mix well. Stir and cook the mixture for 5 minutes until the beef is done. Serve warm.

Beef Lo Mein

Preparation time: 10 minutes

Cook time: 20 minutes

Nutrition facts (per serving): 357 Cal (24g fat, 32g protein, 0g fiber)

Have you ever tried making the beef lo Mein at home? Well, here's a recipe to make some by yourself. Enjoy them with some fresh salad.

Ingredients (4 servings)

Beef and marinade

12 oz. flank steak, sliced

1 teaspoon cornstarch

1 teaspoon soy sauce

1 teaspoon vegetable oil

¼ teaspoon baking soda

Sauce

1 tablespoon light soy sauce

1 tablespoon oyster sauce

2 teaspoons dark soy sauce

½ teaspoon sesame oil

½ teaspoon salt

¼ teaspoon sugar

¼ teaspoon white pepper

Noodles

1-lb. fresh lo Mein noodles, boiled

1 garlic clove, minced

1 carrot, julienned

½ red bell pepper, julienned

½ cup mushrooms, sliced

½ cup bamboo shoots, sliced

2 cups Napa cabbage, shredded

⅔ cup snow peas

2 cups mung bean sprouts

2 tablespoons vegetable oil

1 tablespoon Shaoxing wine

2 scallions, julienned

Preparation

Mix the soy sauce and all the ingredients for the sauce in a bowl. Coat the beef cubes with cornstarch, soy sauce, and baking soda. Sear the beef with vegetable oil in a skillet until golden brown. Sauté the ginger, carrot, cabbage, bell pepper, mushrooms, snow peas, bean sprouts, wine, scallion, and garlic with oil in a suitable wok for 7 minutes. Add the beef cubes and the sauce into the wok and then mix well. Stir and cook the mixture for 5 minutes until the beef is done. Serve warm.

Chinese Fried Ribs

Preparation time: 15 minutes
Cook time: 20 minutes
Nutrition facts (per serving): 493 Cal (15g fat, 30g protein, 1.7g fiber)

A perfect mix of pork ribs with bean curd is a must to try. Serve warm with your favorite side salad for the best taste.

Ingredients (4 servings)

2 lbs. pork ribs, cut into 1- inch nuggets
1 large piece red fermented bean curd
½ teaspoon ground white pepper
1 teaspoon sesame oil
1 teaspoon five-spice powder
2 tablespoons Shaoxing wine
1 tablespoon soy sauce
1 tablespoon maple syrup
½ teaspoon garlic powder
½ teaspoon onion powder
½ teaspoon baking soda
¼ cup cornstarch
3 cups canola oil

Preparation

Mix the bean curd, white pepper, sesame oil, spice powder, wine, soy sauce, maple syrup, garlic powder, onion powder, baking soda, and cornstarch in a bowl. Stir in the pork ribs and mix well to coat. Cover the pork and marinate for 1 hour in the refrigerator. Add 3 cups canola oil in a deep pan and heat up to 350 degrees F. Deep fry the pork chunks for 7 minutes until golden brown. Serve warm.

Cantonese Pork Knuckles

Preparation time: 15 minutes
Cook time: 2 hours 3 minutes
Nutrition facts (per serving): 357 Cal (10g fat, 13g protein, 2g fiber)

The Cantonese pork knuckles are famous for their unique taste and aroma, and now you can bring those exotic flavors home by using this recipe.

Ingredients (4 servings)

1-lb. ginger
5 cups Chinese sweet vinegar
½ cup Chinese black vinegar
2 lbs pork knuckle
2 tablespoons Shaoxing wine
6 hard-boiled eggs
Salt, to taste

Preparation

Boil the ginger with sweet vinegar and black vinegar in a cooking pot for 90 minutes on a simmer. Add the pork knuckles, wine, and enough water to cover the pork and cook for 3 minutes. Cover and cook for another 90 minutes over medium heat. Add the hard-boiled eggs to the pork and cook the mixture to a boil. Serve warm.

Beijing Lamb Skewers

Preparation time: 10 minutes

Cook time: 12 minutes

Nutrition facts (per serving): 428 Cal (18g fat, 26g protein, 1g fiber)

Have you tried the Beijing lamb skewers before? Well, now you can enjoy this unique and flavorsome combination by cooking this recipe at home.

Ingredients (4 servings)

1-lb. lamb shoulder, diced

2 teaspoons cumin seeds

1 tablespoon dried chili flakes

Salt, to taste

1 tablespoon oil

Bamboo skewers

Preparation

Grind the cumin seeds with chili flakes, oil, and salt in a mortar with a pestle. Rub this mixture over the lamb cubes and cover it to marinate for 30 minutes. Thread the lamb cubes on the skewers. Grill the lamb skewers for 6 minutes in the preheated grill over medium heat per side. Enjoy.

Xinjiang Cumin Lamb

Preparation time: 15 minutes
Cook time: 20 minutes
Nutrition facts (per serving): 352 Cal (24g fat, 31g protein, 0.6g fiber)

This Xinjiang cumin lamb meal is so delicious and perfect to complete your menu, and this one, in particular, is great to have on a nutritious diet. It's best to serve a large number of guests.

Ingredients (4 servings)
Lamb marinade
1-lb. lamb shoulder, cut into 2-inch pieces

1 tablespoon cumin

1 ½ teaspoon cornstarch

1 tablespoon oil

1 tablespoon light soy sauce

1 tablespoon Shaoxing rice wine

Dish
2 tablespoons cumin seeds

2 tablespoons oil

2 red chili peppers, chopped

½ teaspoon Sichuan red pepper flakes

¼ teaspoon sugar

2 scallions, chopped

Large handful of chopped cilantro

Salt, to taste

Preparation

Mix the soy sauce, cornstarch, wine, and cumin in a bowl and toss in the lamb pieces. Cover and marinate for 1 hour in the refrigerator. Add the oil and the marinated lamb to a skillet and then sear for minutes per side. Mix chili peppers, Sichuan red pepper flakes, sugar, scallions, cilantro, salt, cumin seeds, and oil in a suitable wok. Sauté for 1 minute and then add the seared lamb to the wok. Continue cooking the lamb for 5 minutes. Serve warm.

Xinjiang Lamb Rice

Preparation time: 15 minutes
Cook time: 33 minutes
Nutrition facts (per serving): 357 Cal (9g fat, 24g protein, 3g fiber)

Now you can quickly make flavorsome lamb rice at home and serve it to have a fancy meal for yourself and your guest.

Ingredients (4 servings)

2 cups uncooked white rice

2 lbs. fatty lamb, cut into chunks

4 cups of water

3 ginger slices

3 tablespoons oil

1 medium onion, diced

2 teaspoons salt

2 teaspoons soy sauce

1 teaspoon cumin powder

1-lb. carrots, cut into thin strips

¼ cup raisins

Preparation

Sauté the onion, ginger, and carrots with oil in a cooking pot for 5 minutes until soft. Stir in the lamb, salt, soy sauce, cumin powder and then sauté for 8 minutes. Add water to the lamb and bring it to a boil. Stir in the rice, cover, and cook for 15 minutes on medium-high heat. Add raisins to the rice and mix well. Cook for 5 minutes, then serve warm.

Xi'an Cumin Lamb Burgers

Preparation time: 10 minutes
Cook time: 20 minutes
Nutrition facts (per serving): 416 Cal (8g fat, 27g protein, 1g fiber)

Let's make some cumin lamb burgers with these simple ingredients. Mix them together and then cook to have a great combination of flavors.

Ingredients (6 servings)

1 tablespoon cumin seeds
1 teaspoon Sichuan peppercorns
½ teaspoon red chili flakes
1-lb. ground lamb
1 teaspoon salt
1 medium red onion, sliced
1 jalapeno, sliced
1 small red bell pepper, sliced
1 tablespoon vegetable oil
1 cup plain Greek Yogurt
2 garlic cloves, minced
4 Brioche or Potato buns
1 cucumber, diced

Preparation

Toast the peppercorns, cumin seeds, and red chili flakes in a skillet. Transfer the mixture to a pestle and grind with a mortar. Mix the lamb with half of the toasted spice mixture and salt and make 4 patties from it. Set an iron skillet with oil on medium heat and sear the patties for 2 minutes per side. Transfer the patties to a plate and keep them covered aside. Add the peppers and onion to the skillet until caramelized. Mix the yogurt with salt, garlic, and the remaining spice mixture in a bowl. Place one patty in each bun and then divide the caramelized onion, cucumber, and yogurt sauce on the burgers. Serve.

Chinese Braised Lamb Bake

Preparation time: 10 minutes
Cook time: 1 hour 27 minutes
Nutrition facts (per serving): 326 Cal (17g fat, 23g protein, 2g fiber)

This braised lamb bake will melt your heart away with its epic flavors. The lamb is cooked with bean curd and lots of sauces to make it taste even better and more nutritious.

Ingredients (4 servings)
2 ½ lbs. boneless lamb meat, diced
15 ginger slices
2 tablespoons oil
6 scallions
½ teaspoon rock sugar
3 pieces fermented red bean curd
¼ cup Zhu Hou sauce
1-star anise
3 tablespoons Shaoxing wine
1 teaspoon dark soy sauce
2 tablespoons light soy sauce
2 tablespoons oyster sauce
1 dried tangerine peel
6 dried Shiitake mushrooms, soaked, and cut in half
4 small carrots, cut into chunks
1 small bamboo shoot, peeled and cut into slices
6 bean thread/sticks, soaked and diced
Salt, to taste

Preparation

Add the lamb and 4 slices of ginger to a cooking pan and fill it with water. Boil the lamb, then drain, and rinse under cold water. Sauté the ginger and scallions with 2 tablespoons oil in a suitable wok. Stir in the sugar, red bean curd, and Zha hot sauce. Next, cook for 5 minutes. Add the lamb, star anise, wine, soy sauces, oyster sauce, mushroom water, and mushrooms. Then add enough water to cover all the ingredients. Cover and cook the lamb mixture for 60 minutes. Add the bamboo shoots, bean threads, and carrot and then cook for 20 minutes. Serve warm.

Yaki Udon

Preparation time: 10 minutes

Cook time: 16 minutes

Nutrition facts (per serving): 379 Cal (18g fat, 21g protein, 6g fiber)

This Yaki Udon recipe has unique flavors due to its rich mix of Udon noodles with mushrooms, pork, and other veggies. Serve warm with your favorite greens on the side.

Ingredients (6 servings)

1-lb. frozen Udon noodles

2 tablespoons butter

1 garlic clove, minced

2 teaspoons dashi powder

1 tablespoon oil

4 oz. pork shoulder

4 oz. oyster mushrooms, sliced

2 tablespoons mirin

2 cups cabbage, shredded

1 medium carrot, julienned

⅛ teaspoon black pepper

2 tablespoons soy sauce

1 tablespoon water

2 scallions, julienned

Preparation

Boil the dry noodles in hot water as per the package's instructions and then drain. Sauté the garlic with butter in a Dutch oven for 30 seconds. Stir in the pork shoulder and then sauté for 5 minutes. Add the mushrooms, along with the remaining ingredients, except for the noodles. Cover and cook for 10 minutes until pork is tender. Stir in the noodles and mix well. Serve warm.

Asian Garlic Noodles

Preparation time: 15 minutes
Cook time: 10 minutes
Nutrition facts (per serving): 293 Cal (13g fat, 14g protein, 7g fiber)

If you haven't tried the Asian Garlic noodles, then here comes a simple and easy to cook recipe that you can recreate at home in no time with minimum efforts.

Ingredients (4 servings)

12 oz. thin spaghetti

4 tablespoons unsalted butter

8 garlic cloves, peeled and sliced

⅛ teaspoon turmeric

1 tablespoon oyster sauce

1 tablespoon soy sauce

1 teaspoon brown sugar

1 teaspoon sesame oil

1 whole scallion, chopped

¼ cup Parmesan cheese

Preparation

Boil the spaghetti in hot water as per the package's instructions and then drain. Sauté the garlic with butter in a suitable wok oven for 30 seconds. Mix the turmeric, soy sauce, oyster sauce, brown sugar, sesame oil, scallions and Parmesan cheese in a bowl. Pour this mixture into the wok and cook for 30 seconds. Toss in the boiled spaghetti and mix well with the sauce. Serve warm.

Spicy Cold Noodles (Liangpi)

Preparation time: 15 minutes

Cook time: 20 minutes

Nutrition facts (per serving): 319cal (14g fat, 18g protein, 7g fiber)

Chinese Cold noodles or Liangpi is one option to go for. Plus, if you have bean sprouts and some Liangpi noodles at home, then you can make it in no time.

Ingredients (4 servings)

Sauce

¼ cup chili oil

2 teaspoons Chinese black vinegar

1 tablespoon light soy sauce

1 teaspoon sesame oil

1 tablespoon toasted sesame seeds

1 teaspoon Sichuan peppercorn powder

½ teaspoon sugar

¼ teaspoon salt

2 garlic cloves, minced

Dish

8 oz. fresh Liangpi noodles

1 ½ cups bean sprouts

4 oz. wheat gluten

¼ cup cilantro leaves

1 small cucumber, julienned

Preparation

Boil the dry noodles in hot water as per the package's instructions and then drain. Mix all the ingredients for the liquid sauce in a small bowl. Pour this sauce into a wok and cook for 30 seconds. Stir in the bean sprouts, wheat gluten, cucumber, and cilantro leaves. Mix well, then add the noodles, and cook for 1 minute. Serve warm.

Peanut Butter Noodles

Preparation time: 10 minutes
Cook time: 20 minutes
Nutrition facts (per serving): 402 Cal (21g fat, 12g protein, 5g fiber)

The peanut butter noodles are enjoyed with mixed roasted veggies, and they taste great. Have them at your dinner table for a tempting serving.

Ingredients (4 servings)

7 oz. fresh white noodles
2 garlic cloves, minced
1 ½ teaspoon ginger, minced
⅓ cup peanut butter
2-3 tablespoons hot water
1 tablespoon Thai black soy sauce
2 teaspoons light soy sauce
2 teaspoons fish sauce
½ teaspoon sesame oil
1 tablespoon lime juice
2 teaspoons chili oil

Preparation

Boil the dry noodles in hot water as per the package's instructions and then drain. Sauté the garlic and ginger with peanut butter in a suitable wok for 30 seconds. Stir in all the sauces, water, lime juice, and chili oil. Mix well and cook it for 1 minute and then toss in the noodles. Mix well and serve warm.

Shrimp Noodles

Preparation time: 5 minutes
Cook time: 30 minutes
Nutrition facts (per serving): 376 Cal (14g fat, 22g protein, 18g fiber)

This noodle recipe will make your day with its delightful taste. Serve warm with your favorite salad and chili sauce.

Ingredients (4 servings)

5 oz. dried vermicelli rice noodles
12 frozen shrimp, peeled, deveined, and butterflied
2 ½ tablespoon vegetable oil
2 eggs, beaten
2 garlic cloves, chopped
4 oz. char Siu, Chinese Roast Pork
3 dried red chili peppers
9 oz. Napa cabbage, shredded
1 medium carrot
1 tablespoon Shaoxing wine
2 tablespoons curry powder
2 teaspoons salt
¼ teaspoon sugar
⅛ teaspoon white pepper
4 tablespoons chicken stock
1 tablespoon vegetable oil
½ teaspoon sesame oil
1 ½ teaspoons soy sauce
1 scallion, julienned
½ cored onion, sliced

Preparation

Boil the dry noodles in hot water as per the package's instructions and then drain. Sauté the garlic with oil in a suitable wok for 30 seconds. Stir in the cabbage, carrot, and onion and then sauté for 5 minutes. Add the shrimp and the rest of the ingredients, except the noodles. Cover and cook for 2 minutes until the shrimp turn white. Stir in the noodles and mix well. Serve warm.

Chicken Mei Fun

Preparation time: 15 minutes
Cook time: 30 minutes
Nutrition facts (per serving): 477 Cal (24g fat, 30g protein, 3g fiber)

If you want some new and exotic flavors in your meals, then this chicken Mei un recipe is best to bring that variety to the menu.

Ingredients (4 servings)
Rice noodles
7 oz. dried rice vermicelli noodles

1 teaspoon vegetable oil

½ teaspoon dark soy sauce

Chicken
7 oz. chicken breast, cut into strips

1 teaspoon cornstarch

1 tablespoon water

1 ½ teaspoon oyster sauce

2 teaspoons Shaoxing wine

¼ teaspoon white pepper

1 pinch five spice powder

1 teaspoon vegetable oil

Dish
2 ginger slices, julienned

4-5 small shallots, sliced

1 medium carrot, julienned

5 oz. cabbage, shredded

3 scallions, cut into 2-inch pieces

3 tablespoons vegetable oil

1 ½ tablespoon light soy sauce

½ teaspoon sesame oil

¼ teaspoon white pepper

Salt, to taste

2 tablespoons water

Preparation

Boil the dry noodles in hot water as per the package's instructions and then drain. Sauté the noodles with oil and soy sauce in a skillet and keep it aside. Mix the chicken with the cornstarch, water, oyster sauce, wine, spice powder, and white pepper in a bowl. Heat oil in a suitable wok and sear the chicken over medium heat until golden brown. Stir in the shallots, carrots, and cabbage and then sauté for 3 minutes. Toss in the rest of the ingredients along with the noodles and then mix well. Serve warm.

Chinese Sausage Fried Rice

Preparation time: 10 minutes
Cook time: 10 minutes
Nutrition facts (per serving): 492 Cal (39g fat, 32g protein, 1.2g fiber)

Here's classic Chinese sausage fried rice for your dinner and lunch. Serve it with a delicious salad and enjoy the best of it.

Ingredients (4 servings)
3 Chinese sausages, diced
1 medium onion, chopped
5 cups cooked white rice
¾ teaspoon salt
¼ teaspoon sugar
2 teaspoons hot water
¼ teaspoon sesame oil
1 teaspoon soy sauce
½ teaspoon dark soy sauce
⅛ teaspoon white pepper
3 tablespoons vegetable oil
2 eggs, beaten
⅔ cup of frozen green peas
1 cup mung bean sprouts, boiled
2 scallions, chopped
1 teaspoon Shaoxing wine

Preparation

Sauté the onion with oil in a cooking pot for 2 minutes. Stir in the sausages, bean sprouts, eggs, all the sauces, sugar, spices, and peas. Mix well and cook for 5 minutes with occasional stirring. Stir in the rice and scallions and then mix well. Serve warm.

Pork Fried Rice

Preparation time: 15 minutes

Cook time: 12 minutes

Nutrition facts (per serving): 392 Cal (18g fat, 29g protein, 1g fiber)

Are you in a mood to have pork fried rice on the menu? Well, you can try this pork mixed with rice for a change and see how tasty it is.

Ingredients (4 servings)

1 tablespoon hot water

1 teaspoon honey

1 teaspoon sesame oil

1 teaspoon Shaoxing wine

1 tablespoon soy sauce

1 teaspoon dark soy sauce

¼ teaspoon white pepper

5 cups cooked Jasmine rice

1 tablespoon oil

1 medium onion, diced

1-lb. Chinese BBQ pork, diced

1 teaspoon salt

½ cup bean sprouts

2 eggs, scrambled

2 scallions, chopped

Preparation

Sauté the onion, bean sprouts, and pork with oil in a cooking pot for 7 minutes. Stir in the rest of the ingredients, along with the eggs, except for the rice. Mix well and cook for 5 minutes. Stir in the rice and mix gently. Serve warm.

Braised Duck with Taro

Preparation time: 10 minutes
Cook time: 30 minutes
Nutrition facts (per serving): 344 Cal (41g fat, 34g protein, 3g fiber)

Try the Chinese Braised Duck with Taro and cook it quickly to serve at your dinner table. Serve this duck with sautéed asparagus and mushrooms.

Ingredients (8 servings)

4 lbs. duck, cut into pieces

1 ½ lbs. large taro

½ cup oil

1 small piece of rock sugar

5 ginger slices

8 garlic cloves, smashed

3 scallions, white and green parts separated

¼ cup Shaoxing wine

1 tablespoon oyster sauce

3 tablespoons light soy sauce

2 tablespoons dark soy sauce

2 cups of water

Preparation

Sauté the ginger, garlic, scallions, and oil in a cooking pan. Stir in the wine, oyster sauce, soy sauce, water, sugar, and duck to the pan. Sear the duck for 3 minutes and then pour in the water. Cover and cook the duck for 20 minutes on medium-low heat. Stir in the taro and cook for 7 minutes. Serve warm.

Chicken Egg Foo Young

Preparation time: 15 minutes

Cook time: 21 minutes

Nutrition facts (per serving): 309 Cal (12g fat, 27g protein, 3g fiber)

Do you want to enjoy the famous Egg Foo Young? Then try this recipe and enjoy the best of all flavors in one single meal.

Ingredients (2 servings)

Pancakes

10 oz. chicken mince

1 tablespoon water

1 teaspoon soy sauce

2 teaspoons cornstarch

1 tablespoon peanut oil

1 medium onion, diced

2 cups mung bean sprouts, boiled

6 large eggs

¼ teaspoon sesame oil

1 scallion, chopped

Sesame seeds

Gravy

1 tablespoon vegetable oil

1 tablespoon flour

½ teaspoon turmeric

½ teaspoon paprika

⅛ teaspoon garlic powder

⅛ teaspoon onion powder

3 cups chicken stock

2 teaspoons soy sauce

1 tablespoon oyster sauce

½ teaspoon sesame oil

¼ teaspoon white pepper

¼ cup cornstarch

Salt, to taste

¼ cup chicken stock

Preparation

Mix the chicken cubes with 1 tablespoon water, 1 teaspoon cornstarch, and 1 teaspoon soy sauce in a bowl. Cover and keep it aside. Prepare the sauce, add oil to a medium pot, and stir in 1 tablespoon flour. Stir and cook this mixture for 20 seconds and then stir in the paprika, turmeric, onion powder, and garlic powder. Mix and cook for 15 seconds and then add chicken stock. Cook this mixture to a simmer and then add sesame oil, oyster sauce, white pepper, and soy sauce. Cook and mix this sauce for 30 seconds. Add 1 tablespoon oil and chicken cubes in a skillet until golden brown. Mix the bean sprouts with onion, chicken, eggs, and cornstarch in a bowl. Make medium-sized patties from this mixture. Set a skillet over medium heat and pour in sesame oil. Sear the patties for 5 minutes per side until golden brown. Pour the prepared sauce on top of the patties. Serve warm.

Chicken and Broccoli with Brown Sauce

Preparation time: 15 minutes
Cook time: 20 minutes
Nutrition facts (per serving): 400 Cal (11g fat, 25g protein, 4g fiber)

The saucy chicken broccoli with brown sauce will melt your heart with its great taste and texture. Serve warm with white rice.

Ingredients (2 servings)
Chicken
12 oz. boneless skinless chicken breast

3 tablespoons water

1 tablespoon oyster sauce

1 teaspoon cornstarch

1 ½ teaspoon vegetable oil

Dish
⅔ cup chicken stock, warmed

1 ½ teaspoon sugar

1 ½ tablespoon soy sauce

2 teaspoons dark soy sauce

1 tablespoon oyster sauce

1 teaspoon sesame oil

⅛ teaspoon white pepper

4 cups broccoli florets

3 tablespoons vegetable oil

2 garlic cloves, minced

¼ teaspoon fresh ginger, grated

1 tablespoon Shaoxing wine

2 tablespoons cornstarch

2 tablespoons water

Preparation

Mix the chicken with water, cornstarch, oyster sauce, and vegetable oil in a bowl. Prepare the sauce by mixing chicken stock with oyster sauce, soy sauce, white pepper, and sesame oil in a bowl. Boil the broccoli in water for 1 minute and then drain. Sauté the chicken with 2 tablespoons of vegetables in a suitable wok until golden brown. Transfer the chicken to a plate. Sauté the ginger and garlic with 1 tablespoon oil in a suitable wok and then add wine. Stir in the prepared sauce, chicken, and broccoli. Mix well and cook for 15 seconds. Mix the cornstarch with 2 tablespoons of water. Pour this slurry into the chicken and cook until the mixture thickens. Serve warm.

Cashew Chicken

Preparation time: 10 minutes
Cook time: 25 minutes
Nutrition facts (per serving): 386 Cal (13g fat, 29g protein, 2g fiber)

Let's have a rich and delicious combination of chicken with cashew and watercress sauce. Cook this meal at home and serve warm with some white rice.

Ingredients (4 servings)

Chicken Marinade

1-lb. boneless chicken breast, cut into 1-inch pieces

3 tablespoons water

2 teaspoons oyster sauce

1 teaspoon canola oil

1 tablespoon cornstarch

Sauce

2 tablespoons light soy sauce

1 teaspoon dark soy sauce

½ teaspoon rice wine vinegar

½ cup chicken stock

1 teaspoon hoisin sauce

½ teaspoon sesame oil

1 ½ tablespoon honey

⅛ teaspoon ground white pepper

Dish

3 tablespoons canola oil

1 teaspoon ginger, grated

2 garlic cloves, minced

½ cup green bell pepper, chopped

½ cup water chestnuts, chopped

½ cup scallions, chopped

1 ½ tablespoon Shaoxing wine

1 cup unsalted cashews, roasted

2 tablespoons cornstarch, whisked with 2 tablespoons water

Preparation

Mix the water with cornstarch, oyster sauce, and oil in a bowl. Stir in the chicken and mix well to coat. Cover and marinate for 1 hour. Mix the remaining sauce ingredients in a bowl and keep it aside. Sauté the chicken with 2 tablespoons of oil in a skillet until golden brown and set it aside. Sauté the ginger, garlic, scallions, red pepper, and chestnuts in a suitable wok for 5 seconds. Stir in the wine and cook for 10 seconds. Pour the prepared sauce and mix well. Stir in the cashews and cook for 5 minutes on a simmer. Mix the cornstarch with water in a bowl and pour into the sauce. Cook until the sauce thickens and add the chicken to the sauce. Mix well and serve warm.

Peking Duck

Preparation time: 10 minutes
Cook time: 20 minutes
Nutrition facts (per serving): 278 Cal (10g fat, 34g protein, 2g fiber)

If you can't think of anything delicious and savory to serve, then try this Peking duck because it has great taste and texture to serve at the table.

Ingredients (4 servings)
Duck
4 boneless duck breasts
¼ teaspoon salt
1 teaspoon light soy sauce
1 teaspoon Shaoxing wine
⅛ teaspoon five-spice powder
1 tablespoon oil

Fixings
1 cucumber, julienned
½ cup cantaloupe, julienned
2 scallions, julienned
3 garlic cloves, minced
3 tablespoons hoisin sauce

Preparation
Mix the wine, five-spice powder, soy sauce, and salt in a bowl. Soak the duck breasts in the marinade for 20 minutes for marination. Sear the marinated duck breast in a pan greased with oil over medium heat for 10 minutes per side until

golden brown. Mix the cucumber with cantaloupe, scallions, garlic, and hoisin sauce in a bowl. Serve the duck breast with a cucumber mixture. Enjoy.

Shrimp Toast

Preparation time: 5 minutes
Cook time: 35 minutes
Nutrition facts (per serving): 353 Cal (18g fat, 27g protein, 4g fiber)

Simple and easy to make, this recipe is a must on this menu. Serve with your favorite tomato sauce.

Ingredients (6 servings)
5 white bread slices, crust removed, and cut into 4 triangles diagonally
½ pound raw shrimp, peeled, and deveined
2 teaspoons lard
4 water chestnuts, chopped
½ tomato, chopped
2 scallions, chopped
1 teaspoon fresh ginger, grated
1 teaspoon Chinese rice wine
1 large egg, beaten lightly
2 teaspoons cornstarch
Salt and black pepper, or to taste
4 cups canola oil

Preparation
Preheat the oven to 225 degrees F. Arrange the bread slices onto a 9x13-inch non-stick baking sheet in a single layer. Bake for about 30 minutes. Meanwhile, in a food processor with a knife blade, add the shrimp and lard and pulse until chopped. Add the water chestnuts, tomato, scallion, and ginger and pulse until combined. Add the remaining ingredients except the oil and pulse smooth.

Spread about 2 teaspoons of the shrimp paste over each toasted bread slice evenly. In a deep skillet, heat the oil to 350 degrees F and deep fry the toasts in 3-4 batches for about 1½ minutes. Flip and cook for about 15 seconds. With a slotted spoon, transfer the toasts onto a paper towel-lined plate to drain. Serve warm.

Kung Pao Chicken

Preparation time: 15 minutes
Cook time: 26 minutes
Nutrition facts (per serving): 392 Cal (9g fat, 31g protein, 4g fiber)

The Chinese Kung Pao Chicken is not only delicious but it also makes a healthy and loaded serving. You can serve it with white rice.

Ingredients (6 servings)
Chicken
1 tablespoon soy sauce
2 teaspoons dry sherry
1½ teaspoons cornstarch
1-pound boneless chicken breasts, cubed

Sauce
1 tablespoon Chinese black vinegar
1 teaspoon sesame oil
1 teaspoon hoisin sauce
1 teaspoon soy sauce
2 teaspoons sugar
1 teaspoon cornstarch
½ teaspoon ground Sichuan pepper
2 tablespoons vegetable oil
8-10 dried red chilies
3 scallions, sliced
1 teaspoon fresh ginger, minced
2 garlic cloves, minced
¼ cup unsalted dry-roasted peanuts

Preparation

For the marinade: in a bowl, add the soy sauce, sherry, and cornstarch and mix until well combined. Add the chicken and coat with the mixture generously. Set aside at room temperature for about 10 minutes. For the sauce: In another bowl, add the vinegar, sesame oil, hoisin sauce, soy sauce, sugar, cornstarch, and Sichuan pepper and mix until smooth. Set aside. In a large skillet, heat the vegetable oil over high heat and stir fry the red chilies for about 30 seconds. Add the chicken and stir fry for about 2-3 minutes. Add the scallion whites, ginger, and garlic and stir fry for about 30 seconds. Stir in the sauce and peanuts and cook for about 1-2 minutes. Serve hot with the garnishing of the scallion greens.

Cantonese Poached Chicken

Preparation time: 15 minutes
Cook time: 50 minutes
Nutrition facts (per serving): 225 Cal (4g fat, 14g protein, 1g fiber)

This Cantonese Poached chicken is one of the Chinese specialties, and everyone must try this interesting combination of a whole chicken with ginger and scallion sauce.

Ingredients (6 servings)
Chicken
3 lbs. whole chicken, cut into pieces
2 scallions, chopped
5 ginger slices, chopped

Sauce
3 tablespoons scallions, minced
2 tablespoons ginger, minced
3 tablespoons vegetable oil
Salt, to taste

Preparation
Add 18 cups of water to a large cooking pot and place the whole chicken in the pot. Set this pot over medium heat and add the ginger and scallions. Cook and boil the chicken for 40 minutes until the chicken is tender. Sauté the ginger with vegetable oil in a large pan. Add chicken to the oil and cook for 5 minutes per side until golden. Serve warm.

Chinese Braised Duck Legs

Preparation time: 15 minutes
Cook time: 1 hour
Nutrition facts (per serving): 265 Cal (13g fat, 23g protein, 0.2g fiber)

You can't really imagine a Chinese menu without having these braised duck legs on it. Now you can prepare them using this simple and quick recipe.

Ingredients (4 servings)
4 duck legs
¼ cup Shaoxing wine
2 cups chicken stock
2 tablespoons soy sauce
2 tablespoons oyster sauce
½ teaspoon sesame oil
¼ teaspoon white pepper
3 ginger slices
3 garlic cloves, sliced
12 scallions, cut into 2-inch

Preparation
Sauté the ginger and garlic with sesame oil in a large wok for 1 minute. Stir in the chicken stock, wine, soy sauce, oyster sauce, and white pepper. Mix well and cook this mixture to a simmer. Toss in the duck legs, cover, and cook until the duck is tender. Garnish with scallions. Serve warm.

Chicken Chop Suey

Preparation time: 10 minutes
Cook time: 20 minutes
Nutrition facts (per serving): 432 Cal (24g fat, 20g protein, 1.3g fiber)

Enjoy this recipe on your Chinese menu. This meal is loaded with chicken, bok choy, and carrots.

Ingredients (2 servings)
Chicken and marinade
12 oz. boneless chicken breast, sliced

3 tablespoons water

1 tablespoon oyster sauce

1 teaspoon Shaoxing wine

1 teaspoon vegetable oil

2 teaspoons cornstarch

Sauce
⅔ cup chicken stock

¼ teaspoon granulated sugar

1 ½ tablespoon soy sauce

1 teaspoon dark soy sauce

1 ½ tablespoon oyster sauce

½ teaspoon toasted sesame oil

⅛ teaspoon white pepper

Dish

3 tablespoons vegetable oil

2 garlic cloves, chopped

4 mushrooms, sliced

½ small carrot, sliced

⅔ cup celery, sliced

6 oz. bok choy, cut into 2" pieces

1 tablespoon Shaoxing wine

¾ cup mung bean sprouts

1 cup snow peas

1 ½ tablespoon cornstarch

Preparation

Mix the water, wine, and oyster sauce in a bowl and soak the chicken slices in this mixture. Whisk 2 teaspoons cornstarch with 1 teaspoon oil in a bowl. Mix the remaining sauce ingredients in a bowl. Add 2 tablespoons of vegetable oil in a skillet and sear the chicken for 5-10 minutes until golden brown. Transfer the chicken slices to a plate and keep it aside. Sauté the garlic with oil in a suitable wok for seconds, add carrots, mushrooms, and celery, and then sauté for 30 seconds. Stir in the bok choy, Shaoxing wine, and then mix well. Pour in the prepared sauce, mix well, and then cook to a simmer. Stir in the snow peas, bean sprouts, and chicken. Mix the cornstarch with 2 tablespoons water in a bowl and pour the mixture into the chicken. Cook this mixture until the sauce thickens. Serve warm.

Char Siu

Preparation time: 10 minutes
Cook time: 50 minutes
Nutrition facts (per serving): 230 Cal (23g fat, 12g protein, 1g fiber)

Crispy and saucy, this pork loin Chinese Char Siu recipe is so full of surprise, and you'll love its amazing taste.

Ingredients (4 servings)

2 tablespoons honey
2 tablespoons dark soy sauce
2 tablespoons hoisin sauce
1 tablespoon sweet rice cooking wine
1 whole star anise pod, crushed
Pinch of Chinese five-spice powder
1 (1 pound) boneless pork loin roast

Preparation

In a microwave-safe bowl, add all the ingredients, except the pork, and mix until well combined. Microwave on 60 percent power for about 22 seconds. Stir the mixture well and transfer it into a large resealable plastic bag alongside the pork loin. Seal the bag and shake to coat well. Refrigerate for about 4-12 hours. Preheat the grill on medium heat. Lightly grease the grill grate. Remove the pork roast from the bag and wrap it in a piece of foil tightly. Grill the wrapped pork for about 50 minutes. Remove from the grill and place the pork loin onto a cutting board for about 10 minutes before slicing. With a sharp knife, cut into desired sized slices and serve.

Eggplant Fry with Oyster Sauce

Preparation time: 15 minutes
Cook time: 60 minutes
Nutrition facts (per serving): 370 Cal (17g fat, 5g protein, 3g fiber)

Enjoy a delicious, juicy, and savory mix of veggies cooked with oyster sauce. Serve with white rice or fried rice.

Ingredients (4 servings)

1 large eggplant, cut into bite-sized pieces

Salt, to taste

2 teaspoons cornstarch

⅓ cup peanut oil

1 small russet potato, cut into ¼-inch pieces

1 bell pepper, seeded and chopped

2 scallions, chopped

2 garlic cloves, minced

2 teaspoons sesame seeds

Sauce

¼ cup vegetable broth

1 tablespoon dry sherry

1 tablespoon soy sauce

½ tablespoon dark soy sauce

½ tablespoon sugar

1 teaspoon cornstarch

Salt, to taste

Preparation

In a large bowl of water, add the eggplant, 2 teaspoons of salt, and mix well. Place a plate over the eggplant pieces to submerge them in the water. Set aside for about 15-20 minutes. Drain the eggplant pieces, and with paper towels, pat dry them completely. In a bowl, place the eggplant pieces and cornstarch and gently toss to coat. Set aside. For the sauce: in a bowl, add all the ingredients and mix until well combined. Set aside.

In a large skillet, heat the peanut oil over medium-high heat. In the skillet, place the eggplant pieces without overlapping and cook for about 2-3 minutes without moving. Reduce the heat to medium heat and flip the eggplant pieces. Cook for about 2-3 minutes or until golden brown.

With a slotted spoon, transfer the eggplant pieces onto a large plate. Now, in the skillet, place the potato pieces and cook for about 2-3 minutes without moving. Flip and cook for about 2-3 minutes, without moving. With a slotted spoon, transfer the potato pieces onto the plate with the eggplant. Remove some of the oil from the skillet, leaving about 1 teaspoon inside. In the same skillet, add the scallions and garlic and sauté for about 1 minute. Add the sauce, stirring continuously until well combined. Stir in the bell pepper, cooked eggplant, and potato. Finally, cook for about 1-2 minutes, stirring continuously. Serve immediately.

Desserts

Banana Fritters

Preparation time: 15 minutes
Cook time: 8 minutes
Nutrition facts (per serving): 360 Cal (14g fat, 8g protein, 1g fiber)

These banana fritters recipe gives you an easy way to enjoy a fancy dessert, and this recipe will let you cook a delicious serving in no time.

Ingredients (4 servings)
½ cup of water
½ cup all-purpose flour
½ cup cornstarch
2 tablespoons milk
1 tablespoon granulated sugar
1 tablespoon butter, melted
4 large ripe bananas, peeled, and sliced
Vegetable oil, for deep frying
Powdered sugar for sprinkling

Preparation
In a bowl, add the water, flour, cornstarch, milk, granulated sugar, and butter. Next, mix until well combined. Add the banana chunks and coat with the mixture evenly. In a deep skillet, heat 1-inch of oil over medium-high heat and fry the banana chunks in 3-4 batches for about 2-4 minutes or until golden brown. With a slotted spoon, transfer the banana chunks onto a wire rack lined plate to drain. Set aside to cool down slightly. Serve with the sprinkling of powdered sugar.

Sticky Rice Balls

Preparation time: 10 minutes
Cook time: 10 minutes
Nutrition facts (per serving): 319 Cal (10g fat, 5g protein, 4g fiber)

Count on these treats to make your dessert menu extra special and surprise your loved one with the ultimate flavors.

Ingredients (10 servings)

3 oz. black sesame seeds, toasted

2½ tablespoons sugar

1 oz. butter softened

3 tablespoons boiling water

4½ oz. glutinous rice flour

4 tablespoons cold water

Preparation

In a food processor, add the sesame seeds and sugar and pulse until smooth. Add the butter and pulse until well combined. Transfer the mixture into a bowl and refrigerate to firm slightly. Place 20 equal-sized balls from the mixture and refrigerate until using. In a bowl, add the hot water and glutinous rice and stir to combine. Slowly, add the cold water and with your hands, knead until a smooth and soft dough forms. Make 20 equal sized balls from the dough. With your fingers, flatten a dough ball into a round wrapper. Place a ball of filling in the center of the wrapper. Gently, push the wrapper upwards to seal completely. In a large pan of boiling water, add the balls in 2 batches and with the back of a spoon, and gently push them around. Cook for about 1 minute. Transfer the balls into a large serving bowl along with some cooking liquid and serve warm.

Chinese Almond Cookies

Preparation time: 15 minutes
Cook time: 20 minutes
Nutrition facts (per serving): 455 Cal (6g fat, 11g protein, 3g fiber)

Here's a delicious and savory combination of almond meal with sugar. All the right ingredients are mixed in a perfect balance to give you a great dessert.

Ingredients (8 servings)

1 cup almond meal
1 ½ cup all-purpose
½ cup sugar
¼ teaspoon salt
1 teaspoon baking powder
1 teaspoon baking soda
½ cup vegetable oil
1 large egg yolk
roasted unsalted almonds

Preparations

At 350 degrees F, preheat your oven. Mix all the dry ingredients in a stand mixer. Stir in the rest of the ingredients and then mix well until smooth. Divide the batter into 1 ½ inch cookies, flatten them, and place them in a greased baking sheet. Brush these cookies with egg yolk and bake for 20 minutes in the oven at 350 degrees F. Allow the cookies to cool and serve.

Fried Milk

Preparation time: 15 minutes

Cook time: 20 minutes

Nutrition facts (per serving): 197 Cal (6g fat, 1g protein, 4g fiber)

If you haven't tried Chinese fried milk before, then here comes a simple and easy to cook recipe that you can recreate at home in no time with minimum efforts.

Ingredients (6 servings)

1 cup of coconut milk

¼ cup milk

3 tablespoon cornstarch

3 tablespoon sugar

2 large eggs, whisked

¼ cup cornstarch

1 cup breadcrumbs

oil for deep-frying

Preparation

Add the coconut milk, sugar, milk, and cornstarch in a cooking pan and cook for 10 minutes with occasional stirring. Spread this mixture in a square baking dish and leave it for 60 minutes. Cut the batter into 3x5 cm strips. Coat each strip with starch, egg, and then with breadcrumbs. Set a deep-frying pan over medium heat and add oil to heat to 300 degrees F. Deep fry the coated bars in the hot oil until golden brown. Transfer to a plate lined with a paper towel. Serve.

Chinese Sweet Potato Dessert

Preparation time: 15 minutes

Cook time: 15 minutes

Nutrition facts (per serving): 265 Cal (12g fat, 5g protein, 1g fiber)

The famous sweet potato dessert is here to make your Chinese cuisine extra special. Serve them along with other candies and cookies.

Ingredients (4 servings)

2 large sweet potatoes

2 inches fresh ginger root, skinned and sliced

3 ½ cups water

8 dried red dates

1 (2 oz.) slab raw brown sugar

Preparation

Boil the sweet potatoes with ginger, dates, water, and brown sugar in a cooking pan and cook for 15 minutes on a simmer. Serve.

Mango Pudding

Preparation time: 10 minutes
Cook time: 10 minutes
Nutrition facts (per serving): 691 Cal (51g fat, 3.3g protein, 2g fiber)

Have you ever tried the Chinese Mango pudding? If not, then here comes a recipe that will help you cook the finest pudding in no time.

Ingredients (2 servings)

½ cup hot water

3 teaspoons gelatin

⅓ cup white sugar

2 large ripe mangoes, peeled, pitted, and sliced

1 cup of coconut milk

Preparation

In a bowl, add the boiling water and gelatin and beat briskly until dissolved. Add the sugar and stir until dissolved. In a food processor, add the mango and pulse until smooth. Add the gelatin mixture and coconut milk and pulse until well combined. Transfer the pudding into serving bowls and refrigerate for about 4-6 hours before serving.

Pineapple Tarts

Preparation time: 15 minutes
Cook time: 45 minutes
Nutrition facts (per serving): 396 Cal (23g fat, 8g protein, 0g fiber)

If you haven't tried the delicious Chinese pineapple tarts before, then here comes a simple and easy cook this recipe that you can recreate at home in no time with minimum efforts.

Ingredients (12 servings)

2 pineapples, peeled and diced
1 cinnamon stick
2 oz. rock sugar
1 clove
7 oz. all-purpose flour
1 egg
½ tablespoon water
3 ½ oz. margarine
¼ teaspoon salt

Preparation

Add the pineapple, cinnamon stick, rock sugar and clove to a cooking pan and cook for 25 minutes until soft. Discard the cinnamon and clove and then puree the mixture. Mix the margarine with flour, egg, water, and salt in a bowl. Knead this dough for 5 minutes, cover, and refrigerate for 30 minutes. Flatten this dough into ¼ inch thick sheet and cut 9-12 rounds using a cookie cutter. Place each round in a small tart pan. Divide the pineapple jam into the dough rounds and brush the edges with egg wash. Bake these tarts for 20 minutes at 360 degrees F in the preheated oven.

Soy Milk Pudding

Preparation time: 5 minutes

Cook time: 15 minutes

Nutrition facts (per serving): 248 Cal (13g fat, 9g protein, 6g fiber)

This soy milk pudding makes an excellent dessert serving! It's loved by all, young and adult, due to its delicious mix of soy milk, milk, and sugar.

Ingredients (4 servings)

¾ cup soybeans, pre-soaked until softened

41 oz. water

2 cups of milk

⅓ cup sugar

6 pieces of gelatin sheets

Preparation

Soak the beans overnight and then drain. Blend the soaked soybeans with water until smooth. Strain the mixture. Mix the gelatin pieces with cold water in a bowl until dissolved. Pour the soy milk into a saucepan and cook it for 15 minutes. Stir in milk, sugar, and gelatin mixture. Cook until the pudding thickens. Pour the mixture into the serving bowls, cover, and refrigerate for 2 hours. Serve.

Chinese Egg Tarts

Preparation time: 15 minutes
Cook time: 30 minutes
Nutrition facts (per serving): 384 Cal (19g fat, 5g protein, 1.4g fiber)

Try this egg tart dessert, and enjoy the best of the savory flavors. The recipe is simple and gives you lots of nutrients in one place.

Ingredients (9 servings)

1 sheet puff pastry, thawed
⅓ cup 1 tablespoon white sugar
⅔ cup hot water
⅓ cup evaporated milk
2 large eggs
1 egg yolk
½ teaspoon vanilla
12 foil tart tins

Preparation

At 400 degrees F, preheat your oven. Set a rack in the lower third of the oven. Mix the sugar with hot water in a bowl. Spread the dough into 12x12 inches sheet and cut 9 circles from it. Place these circles in the small tart pans. Place these pans on a baking sheet. Beat eggs with sugar water, vanilla, milk, and egg yolk in a bowl. Divide this mixture into the tart pans. Bake for 15 minutes in the oven at 400 degrees F. Reduce the heat to 350 minutes, then bake for 15 minutes. Serve.

Drinks

Chinese Firebolt

Preparation time: 15 minutes
Nutrition facts (per serving): 210 Cal (9g fat, 1g protein, 7g fiber)

The Chinese firebolt drink is famous for its amazing blend of cherry grenadine syrup, lime juice, and cola drink.

Ingredients (1 serving)

1 tablespoon cherry grenadine syrup

1 tablespoon lime juice

1 (12 oz.) can cola soft drink

1 strip of lemon zest for garnish

Preparation

Mix the cherry grenadine syrup, lime juice, and cola drink in a cocktail shaker. Garnish with lemon zest and serve.

Orange Oasis Chinese Cocktail

Preparation time: 5 minutes
Nutrition facts (per serving): 122 Cal (13g fat, 3g protein, 1g fiber)

The Chinese orange oasis cocktail drink is famous for its blend of orange juice and brandy. You can prep this drink easily at home with this basic recipe.

Ingredients (1 serving)

4 oz. orange juice

½ oz. cherry brandy

1 ½ oz. gin

Ginger ale

Ice

Cherry and mint to garnish

Preparation

Shake the orange juice with cherry brandy, gin, and ginger ale in a shaker. Garnish with mint and cherry and serve.

Blue China

Preparation time: 5 minutes
Nutrition facts (per serving): 131 Cal (0g fat, 0.7g protein, 1.4g fiber)

Have this blue china drink and enjoy the best of the grapefruit's flavors in this drink. Serve it chilled for a crisp taste.

Ingredients (1 serving)
4 oz. White grapefruit juice
¾ oz. lychee liqueur
1¼ oz. blue curacao
Maraschino cherries

Preparation
Shake the grapefruit juice, lychee liqueur, and blue curacao in a cocktail shaker and serve in a Collins glass with cherries on top. Enjoy.

Shanghai Cocktail

Preparation time: 5 minutes
Nutrition facts (per serving): 120 Cal (0g fat, 0.1g protein, 1g fiber)

Here's a special Chinese drink made from lime rum and anisette, which make it super refreshing.

Ingredients (2 servings)

1 ⅔ oz. light rum

1 teaspoon grenadine

½ oz. Anisette

½ oz. lemon Juice

Lemon wedge for garnishing

ice cubes

Preparation

Shake the light rum with grenadine, anisette, lemon juice, and ice cubes in a cocktail shaker. Serve and garnish with a lemon wedge. Enjoy.

Chinese Dragon

Preparation time: 5 minutes

Nutrition facts (per serving): 112 Cal (0g fat, 0.1g protein, 1.3g fiber)

Made with club soda, melon liqueur, and blue curacao, this beverage is a refreshing addition to the Chinese cocktail menu.

Ingredients (1 serving)

1 oz. Midori melon liqueur

1 oz. blue curacao

Grenadine, dash

Club soda

Preparation

Shake the liqueur with curacao and grenadine in a shaker. Pour into the serving glass and fill the glass with club soda. Serve.

Mandarin Martini

Preparation time: 5 minutes
Nutrition facts (per serving): 116 Cal (0g fat, 0.1g protein, 0 g fiber)

This refreshing sweet and sour martini is always a delight to serve at parties. Now you can make it easily at home by using the following simple ingredients.

Ingredients (1 serving)

⅓ cup mandarin orange juice

1 oz. orange liqueur

2 oz. vodka

Ice

Edible flowers for garnish

Preparation

Add ice, orange juice, vodka, and orange liqueur to a cocktail shaker and mix well. Garnish with edible flowers. Serve.

Sour Plum Drink (Suanmeitang)

Preparation time: 5 minutes
Cook time: 30 minutes
Nutrition facts (per serving): 161 Cal (0g fat, 0g protein, 1g fiber)

This Suanmeitang is a great beverage to serve at any time. It's a unique blend of plums,dried hawthorn, licorice and water.

Ingredients (4 servings)

⅔ oz. dried smoked plums
1 ⅔ oz. Chinese dried hawthorn
¼ oz. Chinese dried licorice
4 cups cold water
4 ½ oz. Chinese brown sugar

Preparation

Add plums, hawthorn, licorice, water, and sugar to a pressure cooker, seal the lid, and cook for 30 minutes. Once done, release the pressure completely naturally. Mash the plum mixture and strain this mixture through a sieve. Allow the drink to cool and serve.

If you liked Chinese recipes, discover to how cook DELICIOUS recipes from **Balkan** countries!

Within these pages, you'll learn 35 authentic recipes from a Balkan cook. These aren't ordinary recipes you'd find on the Internet, but recipes that were closely guarded by our Balkan mothers and passed down from generation to generation.

Main Dishes, Appetizers, and Desserts included!

If you want to learn how to make Croatian green peas stew, and 32 other authentic Balkan recipes, then start with our book!

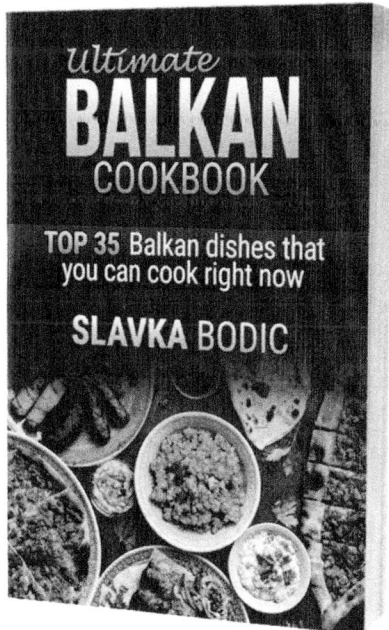

Order at www.balkanfood.org/cook-books/ for only $2,99

Maybe Hungarian cuisine?

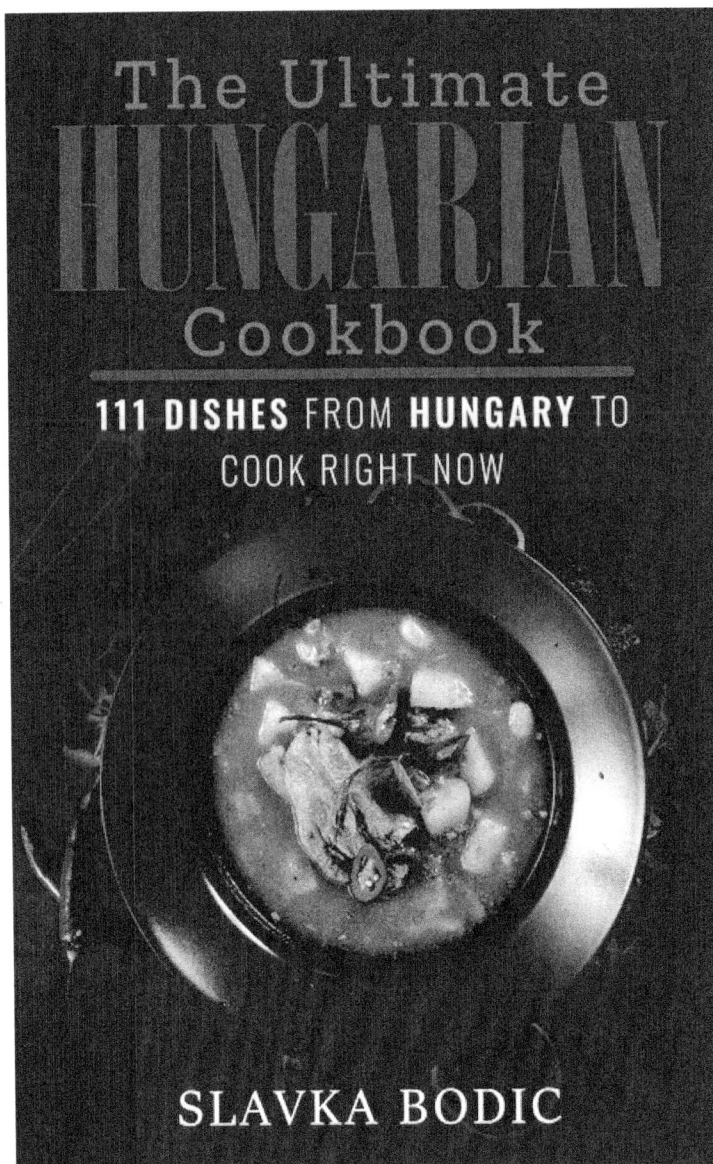

If you're a **Mediterranean** dieter who wants to know the secrets of the Mediterranean diet, dieting, and cooking, then you're about to discover how to master cooking meals on a Mediterranean diet right now!

In fact, if you want to know how to make Mediterranean food, then this new e-book - "The 30-minute Mediterranean diet" - gives you the answers to many important questions and challenges every Mediterranean dieter faces, including:

- How can I succeed with a Mediterranean diet?
- What kind of recipes can I make?
- What are the key principles to this type of diet?
- What are the suggested weekly menus for this diet?
- Are there any cheat items I can make?

... and more!

If you're serious about cooking meals on a Mediterranean diet and you really want to know how to make Mediterranean food, then you need to grab a copy of "The 30-minute Mediterranean diet" right now.

Prepare **111 recipes with several ingredients in less than 30 minutes**!

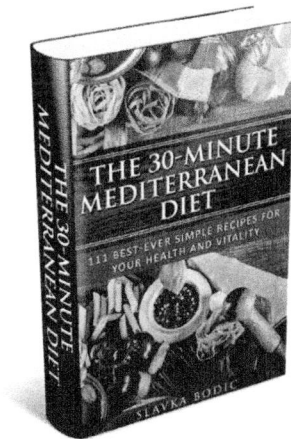

Order at www.balkanfood.org/cook-books/ for only $2,99

What could be better than a home-cooked meal? Maybe only a **Greek** homemade meal.

Do not get discouraged if you have no Greek roots or friends. Now you can make a Greek food feast in your kitchen.

This ultimate Greek cookbook offers you 111 best dishes of this cuisine! From more famous gyros to more exotic *Kota Kapama* this cookbook keeps it easy and affordable.

All the ingredients necessary are wholesome and widely accessible.
The author's picks are as flavorful as they are healthy. The dishes described in this cookbook are "what Greek mothers have made for decades."

Full of well-balanced and nutritious meals, this handy cookbook includes many vegan options. Discover a plethora of benefits of Mediterranean cuisine, and you may fall in love with cooking at home.

Inspired by a real food lover, this collection of delicious recipes will taste buds utterly satisfied.

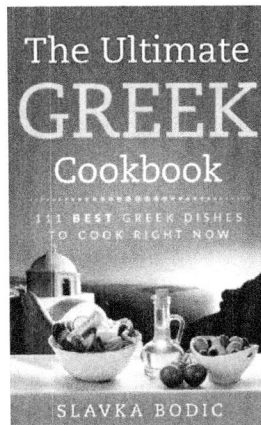

Order at www.balkanfood.org/cook-books/ for only $2,99

Maybe some Swedish meatballs ?

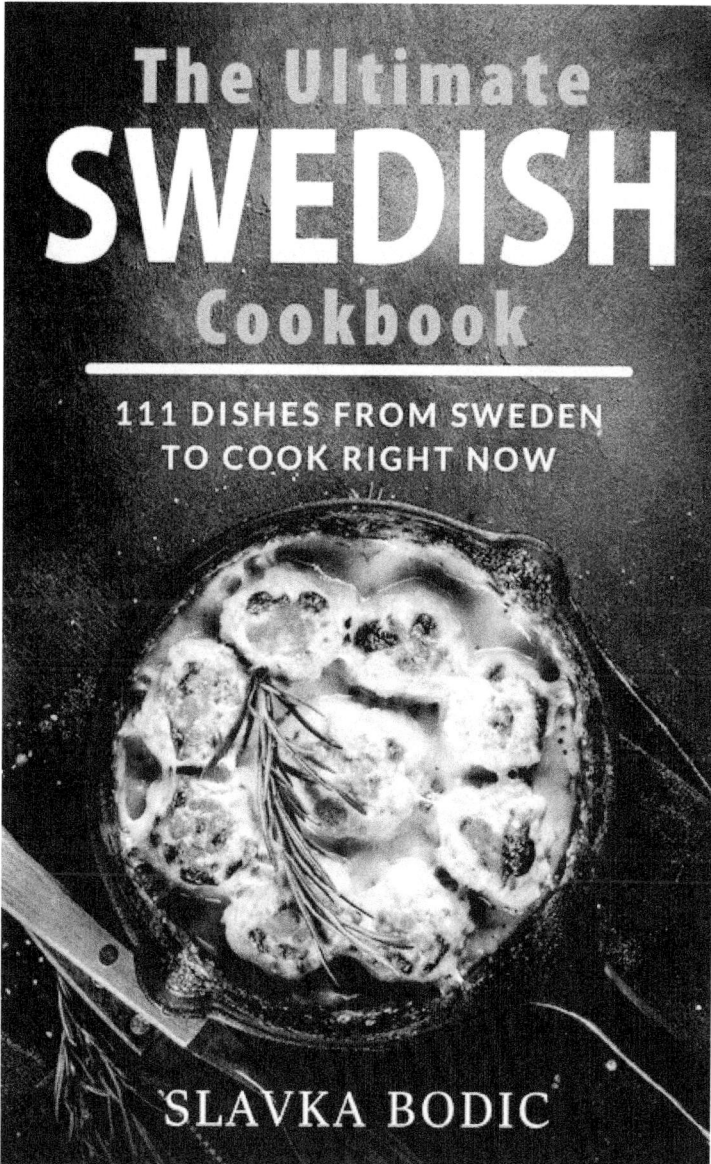

Order at www.balkanfood.org/cook-books/ for only $2,99

Maybe to try exotic **Syrian** cuisine?

From succulent *sarma*, soups, warm and cold salads to delectable desserts, the plethora of flavors will satisfy the most jaded foodie. Have a taste of a new culture with this **traditional Syrian cookbook**.

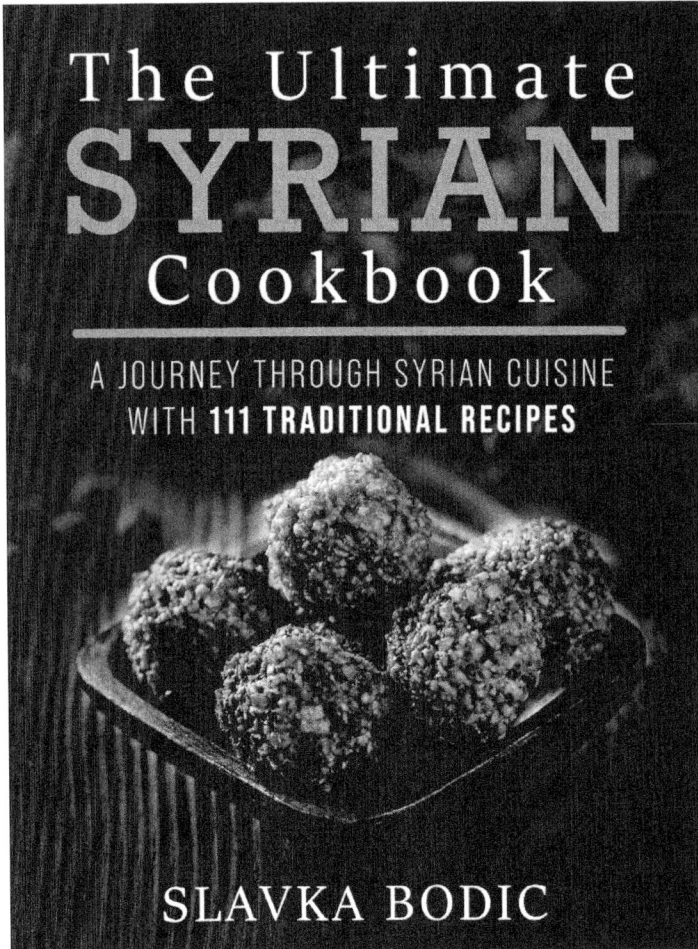

Order at www.balkanfood.org/cook-books/ for only $2,99

Maybe **Polish** cuisine?

Order at www.balkanfood.org/cook-books/ for only $2,99

!

Or **Peruvian?**

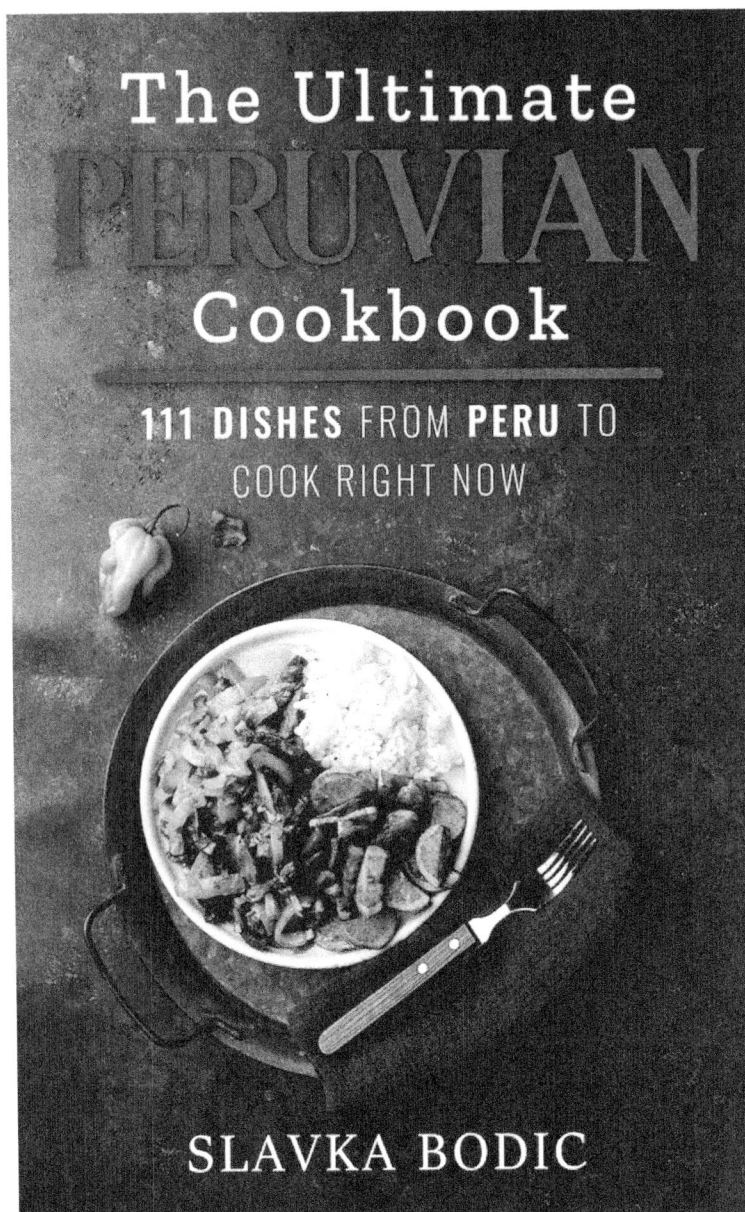

Order at www.balkanfood.org/cook-books/ for only $2,99

ONE LAST THING

If you enjoyed this book or found it useful, I'd be very grateful if you could find the time to post a short review on Amazon. Your support really does make a difference and I read all the reviews personally, so I can get your feedback and make this book even better.

Thanks again for your support!

Please send me your feedback at

www.balkanfood.org

Printed in Great Britain
by Amazon